# Praise for *Clean Language in th...*

What is Clean Language? Essentially, it's a method of c _____ prejudices, allowing the person using it to access and begin to comp _____ that shape the perceptions of another human being. This happens th _____ a particular way, alongside mindful and receptive listening to the r _____ tently, can result in astonishing levels of connection and understandi _____

In this beautifully thoughtful book, Julie McCracken shares l _____ ...ing Clean Language in classrooms and explains how an increased understanding of its potential has refined her practice over the course of a decade or so – teaching her to trust children's resourcefulness; to listen, respectfully and without assumptions; to work with them to create the conditions in which they can learn best; and never to limit them through expectations.

Despite many magical moments, there is nothing fey or romantic about *Clean Language in the Classroom*. It's a practical and methodological guide to a pedagogical approach which, as a parent whose son was lucky enough to spend two years being taught by McCracken, I can confirm is capable of producing incredible outcomes; not just academically, but in terms of the development of the whole child as a confident, thinking, curious individual, always looking for where his learning will take him next.

Helen Mulley, editor, *Teach Secondary*

I love this book for two reasons. Firstly, it is an accessible, humble and practical guide that uncovers a really powerful take on what I have always held to be one of the most important disciplines in a teacher's classroom repertoire – the language used. Secondly, at a time when reductionist behaviour strategies driven by fear and control are the state-sanctioned formula for classroom relationships, Julie McCracken proves that a careful, subtle and humane approach to understanding what is going on in children's heads is not only possible but highly desirable.

Ian Gilbert, founder, Independent Thinking

The power of effective questioning to transform learners' understanding is undeniable. Julie's book provides an outstanding guide for teachers who want to use questioning strategies that have become well established in therapy and counselling to promote deep thinking and reflection. Definitely one for every teacher's bookshelf.

Richard Churches, Principal Adviser for Research and
Evidence Based Practice, Education Development Trust

What's so gorgeous about Julie McCracken's book is not just the practical way Clean Language is introduced and used but also the stories of how children develop the skills to learn together in curiosity and collaboration. This is a wonderful resource for teachers and for their pupils – it brings together a simple tool, innovative applications and inspiring stories. It's a must for any teacher looking to extend their own listening and questioning skills, who truly believes that children will learn what they see and hear.

Caitlin Walker, developer of Systemic Modelling, author of *From Contempt to Curiosity*

At last! Since I first heard Julie McCracken tell her stories of Clean Language in the classroom, several years ago now, I've been looking forward to the day she'd be ready to share them with a wider audience. This book delivers her infectious enthusiasm, her fascinating ideas and her practical tips for applying David Grove's Clean Language. She's used it with young children in dozens of classroom situations, as well as with her colleagues – and for herself.

Judy Rees, Clean Language coach, facilitator and trainer,
co-author of *Clean Language: Revealing Metaphors and Opening Minds*

This book, which is by turns inspirational, funny, heart-warming and thought-provoking, contains all you need in order to absorb clean concepts and put them into practice in your classroom.

Just add curiosity and enough bravery to trust the children (and the process) so that you follow through with your first few clean activities, even when habit is pushing you to take over as 'the expert' in the classroom. You'll soon find that this surprisingly simple yet profound approach really does provide the conditions for children to actively engage with learning, raise the level at which they think and reason, work out how to get past being stuck and develop confidence and self-belief.

Wendy Sullivan, Clean Change Company,
co-author of *Clean Language: Revealing Metaphors and Opening Minds*

This book could – and should – transform the face of education. Julie McCracken has combined her in-depth knowledge of clean approaches and her extensive experience of applying these creatively and effectively in the classroom to achieve extraordinary results. The book is well-written and offers a wealth of tools and guidance. Teachers must read it!

Lynne Cooper, coach, facilitator and trainer, co-author of *The Five-Minute Coach*

During my career I have been privileged to work with many students who have genuinely enquiring minds. It is not always easy to know how to nurture an enquiring attitude – there is often much about formal education that seems to discourage curiosity. How heartening, therefore, to find that Julie McCracken has provided such a readable, practical guide to enabling schoolchildren and their teachers to use the simple yet immensely productive tools of Clean Language. Time and again within these pages Julie demonstrates how the astonishing capacity of young children for enquiry and self-management can be let loose, often by using just one or two questions. Naturally, given Julie's professional experience and expertise, this book is concerned with schools; even so, its contents have the potential to inspire and be applied by educators at all levels.

Dr Paul Tosey, independent consultant, Honorary Visiting Fellow,
Surrey Business School, University of Surrey

*Clean Language in the Classroom* is the first book to describe how Clean Language and Symbolic Modelling can be highly effective in education. It is written from first-hand experience and includes many inspiring examples of how metaphor is vital to learning and understanding. Julie McCracken's trust in her pupils' ability to self-organise shines through, with children as young as five using Clean Language questions for their own and their fellow students' learning. The stories of how this approach helps students overcome their difficulties are heart-warming. We highly recommend this book, not only for teachers but for all educators.

James Lawley and Penny Tompkins, authors of *Metaphors in Mind*

The real beauty in this book is how Julie acknowledges just how big and profound the thoughts of a child can be. Any educator who uses these techniques with this attitude, and excitement about children being generators of big profound ideas, can't not empower them.

Gemma Bailey, Director, NLP4Kids

Julie McCracken

# CLEAN LANGUAGE
# in the
# CLASSROOM

Crown House Publishing Limited
www.crownhouse.co.uk

Published by

Crown House Publishing
Crown Buildings, Bancyfelin, Carmarthen, Wales, SA33 5ND, UK
www.crownhouse.co.uk

and

Crown House Publishing Company LLC
PO Box 2223, Williston, VT 05495
www.crownhousepublishing.com

First published 2016

Front cover image © Vitalinka – Fotolia.com

British Library of Cataloguing-in-Publication Data

A catalogue entry for this book is available from the British Library.

Print ISBN 978-184590860-7
Mobi ISBN 978-184590907-9
ePub ISBN 978-184590908-6
ePDF ISBN 978-184590909-3

LCCN 2015953363

Printed and bound in the UK by
Bell & Bain Ltd, Thornliebank, Glasgow

For Ruby, Kameron, Kira and Max:


Don't limit a child to your own learning,
for he was born in another time.

**Anon.**

# Contents

# Foreword

Some years ago we were part of a team employed to support an underperforming school to turn itself around. Very poor exam scores and behaviour problems meant the school was one step away from being put into special measures by Ofsted.

To start with we wanted to find out how the school currently operated, so one of our team recorded 20 lessons to assess how the teachers taught. She reported that there were only two examples of questions asked to which the teacher did not already know the answer. This made the pupils' answers either 'right' or 'wrong'. The pupils had learned to play the game they called 'school' by trying to guess what the teacher was thinking, rather than developing the skills of learning to think and reason for themselves.

Compare this to Julie McCracken's approach in *Clean Language in the Classroom*. Almost all of Julie's questions can only be answered by the pupils themselves. She listens exquisitely to their answers, especially the metaphors they use. And she accepts whatever is said as an accurate description of their way of thinking – even if spelling a word is like 'frying sausages' or being able to read hard words is like 'a little shiny tickly star in my neck'. Julie realises metaphor is vital to learning, and that once a child has a metaphor for how they do something, they will automatically look for ways to improve it.

This in itself is radical, but Julie goes further. She introduces the principles of self-organisation into her classroom. While following the curriculum, she encourages children as young as 5 to work out for themselves how they are going to do the lesson, decorate their classroom or create a school play. It takes a lot of trust in the pupils' inherent creativity and their capacity to work collaboratively. This trust has evolved from the repeated experience of seeing children individually and collectively prove that they are capable of much more than is generally expected of them.

Julie's book is packed with examples of using a 'clean' approach in education and making it central to all that she does. And while there are other methodologies that have a similar philosophy, her book is the first that describes how to apply the elegance of David Grove's Clean Language and the artistry of our Symbolic Modelling to children's learning in the classroom.

You may start out using this book simply for its clean techniques. However, if you persist, a clean approach may prove so valuable that it will form the basis of your whole pedagogy and become 'just the way we do things around here'.

We wholeheartedly recommend that you apply *Clean Language in the Classroom* to see the difference it makes to your teaching and your students.

James Lawley and Penny Tompkins, London

# Acknowledgements

In bringing this book to completion, I can't begin to express my gratitude for the generous encouragement and support I've received from Wendy Sullivan, Marian Way, James Lawley, Penny Tompkins and Judy Rees. They have championed and challenged me: providing expertise, outstanding feedback and regular nudges ('Where's that book?') through the age it's taken me to write it. They have been sound mentors and remarkable role models. Thank you for sticking with me for the long haul, folks.

I thank Victoria Trott and Phil Swallow who inspired me to begin, Kylie McCracken for her wonderful illustrations, and Jonathan Way, Sonya Smith, Annabel Strachan, Robyn Strachan, Angela Addy and Ruth Huckle for reading and commenting on drafts. Marian also kindly contributed material for Chapter 19 on PE and Ruth for Chapter 20 on music. I thank Geoff Tuff for kindling the spark, for being Geoff and for sharing an infectious curiosity.

Thanks to Graham who has tolerated (for the most part) my long hours on the computer and provided food, drink and chocolate, to my family who have been supportive to the end and have accommodated my 'little obsession', and to Lynn, Lois and Jane for their steadfast support and encouragement. Their critical friendship has supported my development for years.

I send heartfelt thanks through cyberspace to Patricia Shepheard who has been (virtually) alongside me, through long nights into mornings, encouraging me on to the finish line, to Trevor who never once complained, and to my parents who have listened patiently on the phone for hours (days ... weeks ... ) as I've reflected on ideas.

Writing this book has been a delight, an education and a pain. I'm indebted to the many people who badgered me to create it in the first place (you know who you are), to the many colleagues and clients who have influenced my thinking over the years, and to the trainers and authors whose ideas have informed and inspired me.

The staff at Crown House have supported me with patience, kindness and professionalism to bring this book to completion, for which I am deeply grateful.

Every one of you has taught me much about generosity of spirit and teamwork. Thank you.

Naturally, I would like to acknowledge the pioneering work of David Grove. Although I didn't have the privilege of knowing him, he has left such a valuable legacy and the influence of his work permeates everything you will read here.

And finally my thanks go to the governors, staff and parents of St Peter's School in Coggeshall who have encouraged and supported me, and most importantly to the children – co-creators – each one a reason for its existence.

# Introduction

Learning is a private problem-solving process, the student's problem being to create a personal understanding of the skills and knowledge to be learned.

Geoff Petty, *Teaching Today* (2009)

A speaker describes aspects of his spacecraft model while the group ask enquiring questions to elicit more detailed information about it from him. They formulate their questions carefully and wait for opportune moments to ask them. All the while they are listening to the questions of the others as well as to the answers. The group members notice, for each question, whether or not it's effective in unearthing more information about the model.

Some group members offer feedback to fellow questioners, coaching them to improve their performance. The speaker offers feedback too, so that individuals know whether their question has challenged and opened up his thinking. The group discover more about the model *and* more about effective questioning – honing their skills in a collaborative effort.

When questions lead the speaker to 'yes' or 'no' answers, the speaker says so. The speaker then offers the questioner an opportunity to rephrase their question so it encourages further exploration. If the questioner can't devise a more open question, group members offer suggestions.

The atmosphere is comfortable and supportive. No one is subdued or anxious about making unsuccessful attempts at questioning. They know their courage to have a go is held in high esteem by the group. The group ensures that everybody has the opportunity to contribute, taking account of individual interests and comfort levels.

As I sit across the room, apart from them, watching and learning, a question pops into my head and I ask it. The speaker, supported by a couple of others in the group, coaches me to improve the delivery of my question, which becomes more open and effective as a result. When I deliver the new 'improved' version, the speaker offers me the thumbs-up and some verbal feedback before he answers it, 'Good question. It really made me think!'

This is clearly a collaborative learning group. Individuals support each other to develop skills and, in doing so, become more skilful themselves as questioners and as teachers and coaches of *questioning*. I notice they are beginning to distinguish *levels* of thinking, listening and questioning. For example, they are developing hierarchies:

> When you ask about the cat's tail you get more detail about the tail, but when you ask about the cat itself you have to think about the whole cat species and think what kind of cat. You may have to think about the whole animal kingdom!

They contribute to debates about particular questions – take the question, 'And is there anything else?' for example:

> It's a closed question because you can just say 'no' or 'yes' but it still really makes you think, doesn't it? So it's open because it makes you think ... it opens your brain.

They're excited by these conundrums. They muse about questions, their effects and their functions.

These people are 5, 6 and 7-year-old children in a mixed-age infant class-room. They had been using Clean Language for a year and were able to reflect on thinking, listening and questioning with aplomb. They had developed a high level of respect for each other's views and were able to conduct collaborative learning activities independently, interacting confidently with the adults in class as fellow members of the learning team.

A visiting initial teacher training tutor, impressed by the way the children were able to grapple with ideas, observed: 'It's very easy indeed to forget that these are Year 1 and Year 2 children, as their thinking and articulation of it are at the level of older (junior) children ... and that doesn't happen by accident!'

I stumbled upon Clean Language in 2004 and could see potential for an approach, in education, that enables people to lay their thinking out clearly so they can examine it, work with it and share it with others. I could see the potential for myself as a teacher to understand more about my own thinking and learning processes, and those of others, and for my pupils to be able to examine their thinking and learning and their own strategies. We already aimed to do this in schools and a clean approach offered a way to do it more effectively.

Teachers work hard to develop independent and collaborative learning environments and know well the benefits for children. A clean approach can amplify these benefits. On the face of it clean questions are just questions – and simple ones at that – but this belies the depth of thinking and reflection your pupils will experience when you use them.

## What is Clean Language?

Clean Language is a communication process developed by counselling psychologist David Grove in the 1980s and distilled into a model known as Symbolic Modelling by James Lawley and Penny Tompkins in the mid-1990s (see Chapters 5 and 6).

Clean Language is founded on listening and a particular kind of questioning, which uses 'clean questions', formed by taking a person's own words and blending them with a question which has been designed to be as free as possible from assumptions about what the answer might be.

---

### Clean Language is ...

- A set of questions and a particular way of asking them, which directs attention without confining it, limiting it or leading it.
- An extremely receptive way of listening, which remains (as far as possible) free from assumptions, suppositions, presuppositions, opinions and judgements.

### Clean Language helps ...

- Teachers facilitate children to think, without interfering with their thinking.
- Children to become more aware of what they think and how they think.
- Children learn to think.

### Clean Language promotes ...

- Cognitive and emotional development.
- Raised awareness.
- An appreciation of diversity.
- Respect for self and others.
- Self-efficacy.

### Clean Language supports teachers as facilitators of learning

Facilitating is not about transmitting content. Content is developed through the reflections and actions of learner(s), while learning facilitators influence to establish the climates conducive to this learning.

---

If you are going to use Clean Language to its best potential for you and for the children you teach, in addition to learning *how to use it*, you will need to develop an appreciation of *why to use it* and to consider the *contexts in which to use it* for maximum impact. The stories, transcripts, information and exercises that follow will help you, as will reflecting on your practice as a facilitator and reflecting from the perspective of a receiver of facilitation.

# The questions

You are probably curious to know what the questions are. A list of the most commonly used questions appears below. The first four questions tend to be used most often. These form the focus of the seven week journey (see Chapter 2), so you will be equipped with a strong foundation, right from the start.

The bracketed ellipses (...) denote a person's exact words, so their actual words will need to be inserted here when you ask one of the questions.

1.   ... and is there anything else about (...)?

2.   ... and what kind of (...)?

3.   ... and where/whereabouts is (...)?

4.   ... and what happens next?

5.   ... and then what happens?

6.   ... and what happens just before?

7.   ... and where does/could (...) come from?

8.   ... and that's (...) like what?

9.   ... and is there a relationship between (...) and (...)?

10. ... and when (...), what happens to (...)?

11. ... and what would (...) like to have happen?

12. ... and what needs to happen for (desired outcome)?

13. ... and can (...) happen?

There are around 25 additional questions suited to specific contexts which are used much less often and are beyond the scope of this introductory book.

# Where can you use a clean approach?

In classes we've called Clean Language questions detail detective questions (DDQs for short), because when the children first began to use them they soon recognised that the questions elicit more detail in whatever context they are used: from observations of a simple leaf, to pondering experimental design, to a maths calculation, to a philosophical insight, to a social, emotional or behavioural issue.

Clean Language can be used effectively in a broad range of contexts and a clean approach can infuse your classroom with a learning buzz. The following examples will give you an idea of its scope.

Kathy would avoid work tasks using a range of avoidance tactics with her teaching assistant. One day she said she had a tummy ache just as they were about to begin the task. The teaching assistant, starting to tire of Kathy's resistance to work, asked me to intervene. Clean questions revealed that she had a pain, right in the middle of her body, that came when she missed her mummy, and what needed to happen was for her to spend some time each evening with her mummy before she went to bed. What needed to happen for that to happen? To telephone and tell her mummy. I telephoned mum and relayed what Kathy had described. Mum had been busy for a while now but had pressed on with her project, despite feeling guilty about it. That evening she spent 20 minutes reading with Kathy before bed. They scheduled short enjoyable 'together times' every evening. Kathy's tummy aches stopped, her spirits lifted and her work rate improved. You can see that without the questions we would have probably acted on our own mistaken assumptions – and the problem would no doubt have got worse instead of better.

Jim's handwriting was uncontrolled and unreadable. The harder he tried, the shakier his handwriting became. He worked away at fine motor control activities, which were designed to help him, but matters just got worse. Control and fluency in handwriting needn't be just about the hands, of course. One day I asked Jim if he knew any good hand-writers. He said that he did. I asked him to think of each one in turn to get a sense of what it's like to *be* a good hand-writer. With the aid of a few clean questions, Jim identified some common attributes and demonstrated them by answering in actions rather than words. I could see that, for Jim, good hand-writers have a confident, relaxed state, which shows in the way they walk. I asked him to show me how a good hand-writer walks. Jim walked around the room with a kind of cool half strut, half swagger. He practised, taking a few circuits of the room to get into the groove of the 'good hand-writer' walk. Incredible as it seems, within 10 minutes he sat with a flourish and wrote like a good hand-writer. The improvement in his writing was stunning.

John was frequently frustrated. He jumped around the classroom and was often in trouble. Behaviour management helped to lessen the disruption and frustration but it was still a problem, both to him and the rest of the class. When the class modelled 'what we're like when we're learning at our best' he shared how he's like a frog who has to jump from lily pad to lily pad to connect with the learning. When the rest of the class became aware of his needs, they were able to accommodate the jumping around and asked for him to do it in a corner of the class, out of their way. He cooperated with the request and began to jump without disturbing his classmates. The frustration was relieved and the behaviour became manageable.

A class of 5, 6 and 7-year-olds planned, practised and performed a Christmas play for their parents without any content input from me (or any other adults). Clean facilitation helped them to focus on what they wanted to have happen, what needed to happen in each practice session, what happened in each rehearsal, what had just happened (as they reflected on rehearsals) and what needed to happen next to improve performance. The children planned and produced all the scenery and props as well. It was clear that they were organised and on the ball throughout, and they gave a confident, flexible and polished performance. During the rehearsals I didn't have to tell a single child to sit still and be quiet or to pay attention – not once (see Chapter 21 for more on this)!

A 'low-ability' maths set of 7-year-olds were struggling with mental calculations. They were practising using a mental number line. They'd had plenty of experience using physical, written and mental number lines during the three years they had been in school but most were still finding it difficult. I asked the few who were working confidently if they would be happy to share their thinking, so we could all know how they were doing it. I asked Clean Language questions to elicit their thinking processes.

What a surprise! Instead of conventional straight, left-to-right lines (e.g. 0 \_\_\_\_10), they were picturing number lines in much more creative and diverse ways. One child pictured a vertical ladder about 50 cm in front of his face with zero being the bottom rung and the other rungs representing numbers appropriate to the task (e.g. 1, 2, 3 or 5, 10, 15 or 10, 20, 30 and so on). Another child sensed not a number *line* but a series of numbers arranged, as if emerging from his tummy, in a curved, horn-like shape – the higher the number, the larger its size and the higher its location. A third child imagined a line like a long, straight strand of wool with woollen-ball numbers. She imagined a small fluffy kitten pouncing from number to number as she counted forwards or backwards, as though it were pouncing on a ball of wool. As she described it our hearts melted (it's the cutest maths strategy I've ever come across!).

Those who were working less successfully shared their strategies too. Many of them pictured their mental number line running from right to left and were putting all their attention on trying to force it to turn around to match my left-to-right example, rather than using theirs to derive the answer. The children spent some time having a go at each other's strategies, as if they were their own, and discussed which worked well for them and why, and which didn't. Individuals then chose to take on the strategy that was most effective for them (I took on the bouncy kitten). Following this session their mental work became noticeably faster and more accurate, and their confidence and enthusiasm for mental work increased. In addition to any maths gains, these children had become more experienced at thinking about thinking through working metacognitively like this – a benefit for their learning in any subject area.

# Why use a clean approach?

Ken Robinson and Lou Aronica (2009) show us the value of nurturing people's innate nature and Carol Dweck (2007) promotes the application of effort to achieve success. Essentially this book is about neither and it's about both. It's about *emerging* innate nature and how you can facilitate that.

Clean Language can help your students to find out more about who they are and how they can be at their best and to experience the intrinsic motivation and curiosity that this naturally ignites. It helps get to the nitty-gritty to reveal what they know – because minds and bodies hold more information than you might at first imagine and Clean Language encourages that information to emerge.

Human beings are complex systems operating within complex contexts within their environment. Rarely will one discrete cause have a simple and predicable effect. Everything depends – there are so many variables. If I ask John to settle to his work, his response will depend on the nature of the work, the level of his understanding, the quality of our relationship, who is sitting next to him, his parents' attitudes to this kind of work and to school, whether he had a late night last night, whether he has eaten lunch, whether he is hungry or thirsty, what is happening in the classroom around him, what happened just before, what he thinks is going to happen next, the noise level in the classroom, the temperature in the classroom, the space he has for his elbows, his current interests and a whole host of other things.

In teaching, we spend time and attention trying to adapt material to the individuals in our charge. There is a current focus on personalised learning, where children engage with lesson objectives, devise success criteria and monitor their own progress towards outcomes. Children actively and collaboratively assess their work and make improvements as they go. We ask them to share their strategies with each other and contribute to the class learning community.

We promote pupil voice in a variety of ways – by encouraging personal choice and decision-making in class, by supporting children's representation on school councils, by helping children to express views on local and topical issues beyond school and more.

Yet despite our best efforts to engage children and promote independent learning, our attempts are almost inevitably framed within an adult-led paradigm which (paradoxically) works against the good intentions. A clean approach helps teachers to step beyond their own paradigms so they can appreciate those of their pupils and facilitate learning from within the children's own frames.

With regard to motivation, for instance, Clean Language can help children (and you) find and model exactly what they need to motivate themselves. There are many models of motivation and one size does not fit all, but a clean approach offers a bespoke system for each learner, devised by learners themselves.

In the area of behaviour management, there are many successful, well-researched strategies but they don't suit everybody or every context, and most work best with children who present the *least* problematic behaviour. When the strategies don't work with an individual, then what happens? A clean approach can facilitate children to tailor their own solutions (see the example on page 23). As Janusz Korczak (1992 [1925]: 139) observes: 'If the grownups only asked us, we'd advise them correctly ... Why, we know better what bothers us; we have more time to think about and observe ourselves; we know ourselves better ... We are experts of our own lives and affairs.'

We all interpret the world differently. The extent of these differences are not readily apparent in ordinary conversation but are often at the root of miscommunications when we are unaware that other people have different interpretations/meanings/perceptions, and we presuppose that other people's interpretations/meanings/perceptions are the same as our own.

## Practice task

Take a word – for example, 'dog'.

- What comes to mind for you when someone says the word 'dog'?

- Ask four or five pupils what comes to mind for them when they think 'dog' (elicit the finer details).

- Compare their responses.

You will find that everyone has a different interpretation of the word (e.g. size, shape, colour, location, movement, context, single, member of a pack, their emotional response and relationship to it). Some differences may be obvious, some subtle and some hidden until you draw out the fine details.

Knowing that we all have different models of the world, the challenge is one of communication. We so often imagine that we know what pupils (or colleagues) mean by the words they say or the actions they take or the attitudes they adopt (and vice versa).

So how does a teacher take account of individual differences when it's clear they can't actually know what the differences are? A clean approach works to unveil those idiosyncratic ways of thinking and experiencing so we can be aware of them in ourselves and in others. When we're aware of them we can find more effective ways to connect. All good teachers do this in some measure but:

- Without using Clean Language they are not able to prevent themselves from unintentionally 'contaminating' children's thinking.

- Without using Symbolic Modelling (see Chapter 5) they won't get beneath the surface of children's thinking to the depth of idiosyncratic structures, processes and metaphorical thinking which underpin each child's learning and not learning.

- Without embracing a clean approach (see the section on clean philosophy on page 20), they will find it difficult to work with the wholehearted trust of the children and the approach.[1]

---

1    With thanks to James Lawley for pointing out the importance of this benefit to me.

# Embracing diversity

Clean Language has been effective in all sorts of ways: helping children with learning, conflict and behaviour management, thinking skills, creativity and confidence. Clean facilitation skills have increased my capacity to respond flexibly in the classroom and brought a renewed sense of the precious beauty of each class member and their unique perspective on the world. There can be no room for bemoaning inadequacies when you are delighting in the gift that is them.

# The role of metaphor

The term 'metaphor' is used throughout this book to denote analogous descriptions generally (e.g. it includes similarities and comparisons such as similes). David Grove noticed that clients would naturally describe their experiences using the language of metaphor. They would describe one thing, their actual experience, in terms of another — for example, 'like in a dark tunnel'. When he directed their attention to the metaphor, shifts and changes would often occur. They might notice a light at the end of the tunnel for instance.

Grove observed that when changes occurred in clients' metaphorical representations like this, they were paralleled by changes in their 'real world' perspective. For example, a client who has noticed a light at the end of a tunnel may begin to feel more optimistic about his situation and behave more positively. How come?

# What's the link between the metaphors we use and our real lives?

When you stop to consider that many, if not most, of our concepts and our thought processes are metaphorical, then you can see how our perspectives, understandings and behaviour are intimately linked to our symbolic (metaphorical) representations.

If you think of learning as a journey, for instance, it may entail a starting point (a location) and an end point (a destination), which you may or may not reach. It might also involve turning points, difficult terrain, an easy ride, the possibility of getting lost, mapping, diversions and obstacles in the way of progress.

If you think of learning as networking (or as building a network), it's different. A network can build from any starting point or from a range of starting points. It can grow in all directions. A network can become richer in both the number and the kinds of connections and may become complex. Networking may entail randomness, growth, cross-curricular working, cross-domain thinking and systems thinking, for instance.

If you think of learning as soaking up like a sponge, it's different again – learning through effortless absorption perhaps? There is probably only so much you can soak up before you become saturated. And then what happens? Different metaphors have different implications for you as a learner.

**Consider these other common metaphors for learning. What might they entail?**

Learning as:

- Filling a container with knowledge.

- Building a machine.

- Tuning a radio receiver.

- Programming a computer.

---

## Practice task

Pause for a few moments and reflect on your own metaphor for learning (if you have more than one, just focus on one for now).

- What are the implications of holding this particular learning metaphor?

- How does this metaphor enable you as a learner?

- How does this metaphor constrain you?

- Does this metaphor serve you well?

## Practice task

Imagine you held a different learning metaphor (choose one of the examples given above or one you recognise in someone else – a pupil perhaps).

- How might this metaphor enable you as a learner?
- How might this metaphor constrain you?
- Would this metaphor serve you well?

## Practice task

Now take on a third learning metaphor.

- How might this metaphor enable you as a learner?
- How might this metaphor constrain you?
- Would this metaphor serve you well?

Metaphors, then, are the essence of our thoughts, and the *particular* metaphors we use structure concepts in ways that constrain thinking. Lawley says: 'And that is both a blessing and a curse. It allows us to take a certain perspective and think things through without getting overwhelmed by options. On the other hand, there will be things we will not see' (personal communication, 2014).

These constraining influences usually go unnoticed, but by using Clean Language, children and teachers can become more aware of the structure of their thinking and build capacity to engage with it – *what's there* becomes more apparent, so constraints become more tangible and can be addressed and appreciated.

# How does awareness of the role of metaphor impact work in the classroom?

Maintaining an awareness of the role of metaphor in learning has important implications for working with children developing key concepts. This is because:

- Children (and adults) often equate their metaphors with reality – not yet recognising them as representations of reality.

- Some metaphors are useful for some contexts and not for others.

- Some metaphors are more useful than others (in any given context).

- No one metaphor works well for all contexts.

- When children understand the nature of metaphor, they can create their own (i.e. for a concept or learning point) and not be reliant on the teacher's or the ones they meet in books.

Teachers can facilitate learning and address difficulties in understanding more effectively when they are aware of their pupils' (and their own) metaphors – and when they are aware of how metaphors work (see Chapters 4 and 5).

## Facilitating learning – inviting attention – constraining thinking

Any teacher knows that simply telling children something rarely results in their learning it. Wouldn't life be easy if that were the case? Telling them *more* (repeating over and over) or *better* (introducing interest, clarity and novelty) may help them commit information to memory, but the learning is not in the telling – the learning happens in the child.

As a learning facilitator, a teacher's role is to create the conditions for learning to happen – to guide children's attention to their own experience and thinking in ways that support them to reflect, and to examine their current thinking, make new connections and potentially shift their perspective. Clean Language offers a model for teachers to take their questioning to the heart of children's thinking – to engage in deep learning (and, for some, transformative learning) and in learning to learn.

All questions compel children to think. Clean questions give them maximum freedom to answer however they want to – to answer in their 'natural' way.

Many, if not most, questions presuppose a particular kind of answer.

Question: How are you *feeling* today?

Answer: I'm *feeling* fine, thanks.

Question: What *shape* is the chocolate box?

Answer: It's a *triangular prism*.

When you ask about a feeling, both you (the questioner) and the recipient expect the answer to be about feeling. When you ask about shape, you expect the answer to refer to shape. When this doesn't happen it can seem strange and confusing to the questioner (although rarely to the answerer).

> Maths: Children in a reception class were sharing strategies for adding 2 and 5. Jane had already demonstrated her method so I turned to the class and said, 'Jane added 2 and 5 like this (pointing to the jottings on the board). Who did the same? ... And who did something different?' Jon, who had been sitting pensively for a while, shot up his hand. He was so keen to share his thinking, I just had to pick him. His answer: 'If God made the world and the universe and everything in it ... who made God?'

If you teach young children, you will probably have your own examples of mismatching questions and answers like this. I call them 'Joyce Grenfell moments' (find her monologues on YouTube – they're priceless!). The point is that most of us, most of the time, presume that an answer should match the question, and when it doesn't, it's perplexing.

Because most people share this expectation, questions act to 'invite' attention and set constraints, which influence responses – even the most open questions influence recipients' attention in this way. An important skill for success in education (and beyond) is to be able to answer a question *within the frame* of the question (e.g. children need to be able to discern that with 2 + 5 = ? the response will be a number). This ability to discern the frame of a question is central to exam success.

---

## Practice task

All questions presuppose something. When you are asking questions in class, how aware are you of what you are presupposing?

Assemble a small collection of questions that you have recently asked (or intend to ask) in class. For each question consider:

- What presuppositions might it entail?

- How might these presuppositions influence children's responses?

- How might you adjust the wording of the question to minimise (or maximise) the amount of presupposition?

---

# Presuppositions

David Grove wanted his clients to be able to examine their pure experience uninfluenced by those subtle assumptions that are embedded in questions and which lead the recipient to answer in a prescribed modality. He found that questions containing the fewest presuppositions were the ones most likely to keep a person's attention on their own experience and their own thoughts. With these questions, people can respond with information that is true and relevant for them, rather than with information that they may have had to distort to make it fit within the frame of the questioner's own model.

Although clean questions do not 'lead' the answer in terms of modality or content, they do lead in terms of:

- Sequence (timeframe – see page 56).

- Structure (e.g. location, relationship – see page 56).

- Overt use of metaphor (see page 116).

Since the vast majority of people use these to organise their thinking and meaning-making, it is considered 'clean' to do this.

# Parrot phrasing

Grove also realised that keeping clients' words intact when he referred to their experience, or when he constructed questions about their experience, had a similar effect. By 'intact' I mean repeating the clients' words and phrases exactly as they say them rather than paraphrasing them. This is sometimes known as 'parrot phrasing' (Sullivan and Rees, 2008). You will learn how to do this in subtle ways (that don't irritate) in Chapters 1, 2 and 3.

# Symbolic Modelling

In Symbolic Modelling (see Chapter 5) the modeller uses clean questions to elicit information about a person's metaphor and construct a model of it, so that they can ask more informed and targeted questions. This allows the person to examine their own metaphorical constructions (their patterns of awareness) with minimal influence or interference from the questioner but with exquisite precision.

# How does all this apply to classroom life?

There are many ways in which a clean philosophy, a clean methodology (such as Symbolic Modelling[2]) and Clean Language can support teaching and learning. When you adopt a clean approach in your work, you are fostering the conditions for children to reflect on their thinking and their learning processes as freely as possible from insidious constraints – and, for them and you, to witness and work with their perceptions. Clean principles, processes and behaviours used in alignment can create conditions that promote deep learning.

By a clean philosophy, I mean holding the following ideas like an overarching umbrella – one that creates an environment (the principles under which you work) and casts its span over the processes you use and the things you do:

- Trusting that children are resourceful and have in themselves all they need to learn and grow and find their own solutions.

- Respecting individual differences.

- Facilitating from within children's own perceptual frameworks, using the children's own language.

- Working in an information-centred way, in addition to a child-centred or teacher-centred way.

- Accepting information in the form/place you find it.

- Appreciating the metaphorical nature of thinking.

- Valuing pauses as 'response-inviting gaps' where learning/change happens.

- Having the courage to work at your own 'learning edge' (which can be uncomfortable) and being OK with 'not knowing' as you work.

- Realising the immense value of listening and of questioning without imposing your own content.

- Understanding that working with 'what is' and 'what is happening in the moment' is not only good enough, it is usually the best place to be.[3]

---

2   You can read about more than a dozen clean methodologies currently available by visiting James Lawley's blog 'What is Clean Language?'

3   This list was inspired by Grove (1998).

---

## Reflection task

I used the metaphor 'holding ideas like an overarching umbrella', although 'holding ideas like a foundation which underpins all that you do' may work as well or better for you.

What other metaphors come to mind when you think of 'guiding principles'?

What is your *preferred* metaphor for 'working with guiding principles'?

---

By a clean methodology, I mean using the Clean Language questions of David Grove along with:

- A particular way of asking them, including uncommon forms of grammar, syntax and cadence (pace and rhythm).

- Specific processes for using them (such as Symbolic Modelling, systemic modelling and clean coaching).

You will learn how to do this in Chapters 1, 2 and 3.

# Learning to use Clean Language

My experience of appreciating and taking on a clean approach has been an iterative process, and this seems to be the case for most people – a learning spiral powered by experience, action, reflection and dialogue, repeatedly cycling through familiar territory on progressively higher planes. This is not something you can access at arm's length or purely theoretically. You need to engage with it in an experiential way to appreciate its potential. If you read about it without experiencing it you will gain a surface level understanding, which will have value, but you will be missing more than you can imagine.

Having learned to work with clean principles and having developed my own practice, when I then applied it in schools the results confirmed the value of using clean approaches in classrooms. To begin with I noticed that the children (and the adults) I worked with began to tackle problems in more innovative and personally effective ways.

Some examples include:

A student teacher who was experiencing stressful mornings in class. Advice had been offered ranging from practical classroom management techniques, ideas to engage the children and self-help advice about how to relax and de-stress. She was a capable practitioner, her work was good and prior to this she had been highly confident. Nevertheless, it was getting steadily worse each morning. When we met to mull it over she was keen for me to ask her a few questions to shed some light on it.

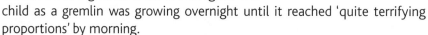

The questions helped her to notice what she was experiencing (an anxious feeling), what that feeling was like, where she was feeling it, what happened just before the feeling and what happened just after the feeling. She noticed the feeling process was linked to her thoughts about one particular child. She realised that she was visualising the child as 'a little bit of a gremlin'. And the image of the child as a gremlin was growing overnight until it reached 'quite terrifying proportions' by morning.

She also realised that these thoughts had been happening for a while, but until now they had been outside of her awareness. Once she knew she was creating the feelings of stress through her own thinking, she was able to take the resultant feelings with a pinch of salt and confidence returned. She began to notice more and more that the child in question was just a child and 'not nearly as scary as the gremlin I've been creating overnight'. The feelings of stress faded away and were replaced by a wry smile as a new-found confidence emerged. She even began to find it funny to think that she had been scaring herself like this.

A child who was behaving unacceptably in school. None of the usual behaviour management strategies had changed anything. A team of adults put their heads together to think of a reward which would motivate him to behave acceptably. In order to work it needed to be something he would want. But despite lots of tempting offers, he wasn't interested in any of the suggestions.

When asked, 'Is there something ... something that can happen in school ... that you would like to have happen, when you *do* come into the classroom on time after lunch (the behaviour the school wanted to see)?', he said instantly, 'Can I play Cluedo?'

One of the adults was concerned that the game would need to be packed away and if this didn't happen on time then the problem would have just translated from one context (coming in on time) to another (packing away on time).

The conversation continued: 'And when you do come in on time and play Cluedo, and you pack away on time, what would you like to have happen?' 'I'd like to choose a friend to play it with and not be told to do it – but for someone to tell me the time so I have time to pack away.' 'And how much time will you need?' 'Five minutes to pack away – and if I don't pack it away on time I can't play it the next day.'

Hey presto, problem solved. This child designed a behaviour management programme that fitted his motivational needs like a glove – and he went on to monitor himself recording successes on a tick list.

An 11-year-old girl who was worried about spelling difficult words in the impending tests. She performed well in class tests but consistently underperformed in what she called 'important tests'. Now, with SATs looming, her stress levels were rising. I asked some clean questions to model what happened when she performed well and she was able to piece together the following process.

First, she would look at a word to be learned and write it clearly, in her mind's eye, on an imaginary piece of paper. Then she would move to another word, continuing on like this until she had a complete list of words on her imaginary page. Then, during the test she would mentally take out her imaginary piece of paper, read it and copy the words on to the answer sheet. This mental strategy was easy and effective for her.

So what happened during 'important tests'? She explained that 'copying is actually cheating', so in important tests she would leave her imaginary piece of paper outside the room. She would 'go it alone' and consequently make mistakes. When I explained that the imaginary piece of paper was a memory strategy and that it was well within the rules for her to take her memory into a test (only real lists of words on real paper are banned), she breathed a big sigh of relief and went on to use her 'natural' visual memory strategy to good effect.

You will appreciate in these examples that the children (and adult) wouldn't have arrived at their tailor-made outcomes if I had tried to instruct or advise them. The final example shows how a clean approach (adopting a non-expert facilitating role) can be used in combination with a didactic teaching approach (an expert 'information providing' role). I did not think for her, or tell her how to learn, or pronounce judgement on her ability or her intelligence. A clean approach helped to elicit precise information about what she was doing and then I was able to provide her with some specific facts, which she needed but didn't have.

In my classes, the children were soon devising outcomes, instead of focusing on problems and ways to overcome them. The children were recognising and responding to their own learning strengths and needs, and those of their peers. From this emerged a sense of 'we' – a learning community – children reflecting on outcomes for the group and responding to the strengths and needs of the group – group self-modelling (see Chapters 9, 10 and 21). That's the beauty of a clean approach: it's both simple and profound. It helps produce tailor-made outcomes that are uniquely suited to the individual, in their context.

You will find stories throughout the book which illustrate attitudes and beliefs about learning, exploring and using Clean Language in the classroom, and how children explore it and use it for themselves. This will give you a sense of what happens when it's put into practice, and what happens next as new ways of working together continue to develop.

In the case studies which follow, you will meet with butterflies, sunshine and beautiful clouds; planets, light sabers and spaceships; fairies, trolls and 'the darkness'. But these are not tales from storybooks. These things are real – they are the metaphors upon which experience hangs. I've changed personal details to uphold anonymity and I've sometimes merged stories into one tale to make a point more clearly, but I've held on to the content so the essence is still there.

Naturally, there were 'learning leaps' and 'plateaus'. I don't want to give the impression that Clean Language is a kind of pink medicine that will cure all your ills with one dose, although at times it can change things for the better surprisingly quickly, as you will see.

I aim to offer my experience and the experience of my classes, so you can take it and run with it, to create learning environments in your own classes, in your own ways, using Clean Language to support truly *personalised* personalised learning – because in the end, the only path you can really tread is your own.

# Part 1
# About Clean Language

# Chapter 1
# Clean Language in a Nutshell

More effort has to be spent in framing questions that are worth asking: that is, questions which explore issues that are critical to the development of children's understanding.

Paul Black, Chris Harrison, Clare Lee, Bethan Marshall and Dylan Wiliam,
*Assessment for Learning: Putting it into Practice* (2003)

Have you ever spent more time and effort than you would like sorting out a dispute between bickering youngsters only to find they carry on as soon as your back is turned? Do you ever tell pupils one thing but they do another, leaving you wondering if you are speaking a foreign language? When you are trying to hold a conversation, or assess their understanding, does it ever seem like you are trying to get blood out of a stone?

If your answer to any of these is 'Yes!' then you are not alone. The reason I've used the clichés above is to illustrate how common these problems are. You may sense an echo of your own teachers, or parents, and realise that they experienced similar difficulties. So how can you shine a light through the fog and connect with children in a way that fosters deep understanding and clear communication in the midst of a busy school day?

In this chapter you will find how you can fine-tune the way you listen to children and how to use clean questions to bring results which will surprise you. Clean Language uses a collection of questions that are as free from assumptions as possible. They will help you to get a clearer idea of a child's thoughts and feelings without 'contaminating' them with your own assumptions or presuppositions.

Clean Language engages children in the kind of thinking which develops their understanding of the external world and their internal world – and it promotes their thinking about thinking. Clean Language questions are definitely questions worth asking.

# Clean Language: a practical overview and quick-start guide

Knowing which question to ask is a skill that can be picked up quite quickly *and* you can develop it into an art over time. Although it requires practice to use the method masterfully, you can achieve results right from the start if you work to a few guidelines. The table below will serve as a navigation aide and as a handy overview.

| | **Clean Language in a nutshell** |
|---|---|
| 1 | **Trust the children**. They can solve their problems themselves given your skilled support. Remember the Pygmalion effect? (If you believe they are capable, then they will be – and, conversely, if you believe they won't, they won't.) It's only natural to be sceptical until you see results and it can be difficult to remain open to possibilities, especially in the early stages, but please don't gloss over this step – it's important. For most people it requires practice. So persevere and work with light, apparently inconsequential content at first – and prepare to be pleasantly surprised. |
| 2 | **Listen, absolutely exquisitely** (see page 35, 'What kind of listening?') to the words the children say and the way in which they say them. Don't make judgements, give your opinion or try to think of solutions – just focus on what they say. |
| 3 | **Repeat back** to them the words they have said (exactly as they said them). |
| 4 | **Ask a clean question** incorporating their exact words: <br><br> • A good question to start with is, 'And what kind of (...)?', infilling the (...) gap with children's exact words. Practise using it until it's tripping off your tongue naturally. <br><br> • An extremely handy question is, 'And is there anything else about (...)?' Practise asking it until it flows as naturally as the first. |

- Add another question, such as, 'And where/whereabouts is (...)?' and practise it as before. Asking 'whereabouts' will ascertain the location of objects or aspects of objects (e.g. the paws on a teddy) as well as the location of feelings or thoughts (e.g. joy, excitement, mental maths manipulations – see Chapter 10).

- Continue adding questions like this (interleaved learning) and you will soon be using more and more of them in your everyday language easily and effortlessly. You will find more questions further along in this chapter.

Note: When experienced clean facilitators review the questions they use in action, of all the clean questions, they find they have used those above more than half of the time. In the classroom, you can explore and augment almost anything the children say to you, in whatever domain, using just these questions.

## Practice tips

- **Ask the questions *exactly* as they have been presented.** The *way* you ask them is important. The uncommon grammar, syntax, tone and rhythm all contribute to the powerful effects of this questioning (see pages 57–59, 'Three-part syntax'). Having said that, you will come across examples in the book where I've used similar (but not identical) questions – losing focus during a fast-paced day does happen. It's not the end of the world, but if you don't ask the questions as presented the effectiveness will be reduced, so try to aim for an element of precision, especially when you are first learning them.

- **Ask with a *clean* intention.** The intention with which the questions are asked is vitally important (clean questions can be used to manipulate, if that is what you intend to do). If your intention is for a pupil to find out something for themselves (i.e. a *clean* intention) then a slight rephrasing of the question will rarely matter much.

- **Ask about strengths and resources: what's going well, what works well, aims for the future and comfortable feelings.** A good rule of thumb is to start by asking a question to which the child will most likely have an answer. More complex and challenging questions can follow later. The questions can invite deep introspection (and they can go deep surprisingly quickly), so avoid asking questions about anything unresourceful, weaknesses or uncomfortable feelings, unless you have had appropriate training.

As leading experts in Clean Language Wendy Sullivan and Judy Rees (2008) put it: 'Go for the good stuff!'

That's it in a nutshell.

As you begin to familiarise yourself with the questions by using them, choose informal contexts to begin with – contexts where individual children are doing the bulk of the talking and where you don't have to focus intently on the content of a lesson (e.g. speaking and listening activities), when children are relating news, during a chat over lunch or in one-to-one conversations in the playground. This will give you an experiential point of reference and a grounding in the questions from which you can develop your skills further by reading on and putting the activities into practice over the next few weeks.

It pays dividends to be able to say the questions out loud in live situations without having to stop to recall them, because once you know them by heart you can focus on applying them with finesse. To help you remember the questions, there is a pocket-sized question card in Appendix A. I don't need to tell you that repetition is the key.

# Chapter 2
# The Seven Week Journey

## A week-by-week guide to using
## Clean Language in your classroom

The seven week journey offers detailed guidance and structure, at a comfortable pace, to fit easily within a busy work schedule. By working through it steadily, you will begin to embed the listening and questioning skills into your daily classroom practice.

I have introduced questions gradually during the first few weeks because my own experience, and that of colleagues learning them, has shown that when you are already working with a demanding timetable, it can take a while to ease yourself into the swing of asking the questions. Once you are asking them habitually, adding further questions will be relatively simple, so I've increased the pace later on. Take it at your own speed. You will have your own best ways of learning, so do whatever works well for you.

Most of the tasks can be carried out as part of your everyday practice in the classroom and as part of your daily contact with colleagues. It will require a level of commitment that will involve more of a shift in attention (a change of focus) than an increase in time.

As you progress through the seven week journey, you will be learning to structure the questions in particular ways, to ask them of unfamiliar things and to use them in new contexts. As well as focusing on the *way to ask* the questions (i.e. how to ask as well as what to ask) you will be considering the *way to listen*.

You may find it useful to:

- Introduce one question at a time – in a gradual way that is sustainable and fits comfortably into your daily practice.

- Practise speaking the questions aloud (using them informally with willing friends, relatives, colleagues, etc.) before using them with the children in class.

- Find ways to experience what it's like to be on the receiving end (e.g. record your own voice asking the questions and use this to ask yourself, have friends/colleagues ask you, have children in your class ask you).

- Learn with other people for moral support, reflective dialogue, feedback and encouragement.

- Remember that what you are learning can benefit the adults you work with too.

---

### Essential tip

Learn the questions exactly as they have been presented. Sometimes people change a word or a tense so the questions fit conventional grammar. Even small changes make a difference to their effectiveness so deliver the questions exactly as they have been designed.

---

If you follow the guidance below you can expect to learn the basics of Clean Language and blend it steadily and seamlessly into your practice in about half a term. Take all the time you need to practise and enjoy the journey.

Here's to you getting started.

# Week 1

## What kind of question?

Let's look at your first question and how to use it. The question '... *and what kind of (...)?*' helps you and the children to think about specifics and to categorise with increased precision. It can also help to get and keep conversations flowing. You can ask this question of just about anything, so you will need to choose what you are going to focus attention on (more about this later).

Notice the question begins with an 'and'. It may feel strange to begin with an 'and' at first, especially if you are working hard to discourage it in children's writing. But it's worth training yourself to do it when asking clean questions because starting your question in this way:

• Helps to soften the question.

• Aids a sense of flow (it acts as a link between the current thought and the one to come) when you are questioning, which encourages thinking to flow.

• Gives the child a little time to begin focusing on what you are about to ask: it acts as a primer.

At the end of the question, insert the child's exact words into the blank space (whichever of their words you have chosen to focus on).

| Example (child aged 4) | |
| --- | --- |
| Question | What did you do in the role-play corner today? |
| Answer | We just played all the time. |
| Question | Oh, played (*said with a curious tone*) <br> … and … what kind of played? |
| Answer | We played shops and added up the money and gave change. |

| Example (child aged 11) | |
| --- | --- |
| Question | What did you do in literacy today? |
| Answer | We just carried on with writing from yesterday. |
| Question | Oh … just carried on with writing … <br> … and … carried on (*said with a curious tone*) … <br> … and … what kind of carried on? |

| Answer | Well, we're writing stories – it's all planned out – but I'm focusing on using paragraphs now, and linking them with pronouns and connectives like 'although', 'on the other hand' and 'meanwhile' … that kind of thing. |
| --- | --- |
| | (This conversation continues on page 40) |

## Task for week 1

As you continue to practise the following questions in informal situations, begin to think about where you might plan to use one or more of them in the lessons you are planning:

- … and what kind of (…)?

- … and is there anything else about (…)?

- … and where/whereabouts is (…)?

## Practice tip

As you get into a habit of asking '… and what kind of (…)?', notice all the things you can ask it of – that is, more or less every word the children utter. Obviously, don't go ahead and ask it of every word as the conversation will quickly turn into an interrogation – be selective.

# Week 2

## What kind of listening?

Now that you are in the swing of asking your first clean question(s), let's consider how you can tune your attention to listen with a more powerful effect (for more on listening exquisitely see page 43–47).

During everyday conversations most people's attention is partially focused on:

- Listening to what the speaker is saying.

- Noticing what the speaker is doing (facial expressions, gestures, etc.).

- Formulating a response to what is being said (deciding whether they agree with the speaker, what they think of the speaker, whether they have had similar experiences to the speaker, on formulating a reply and so on).

If you stop to think about it, when was the last time someone listened to you without interrupting, making judgements or just waiting to respond with their own opinion, answer or idea? Some people, especially some children, have never experienced being listened to with full attention, and for most people the experience is a rarity.

Listening is an absolutely fundamental part of the learning experience. Nancy Kline (1999: 23) asserts that, 'Listening of this calibre ignites the human mind. The quality of your attention determines the quality of other people's thinking.'

Remember, listening is not a passive activity:

- Listening is active.

- Listening is fundamental to the flow of the conversation.

- Listening directly affects the ability of the speaker to think clearly and coherently.

---

## Listening activities

1 | **Listen to a child, friend or colleague without interrupting.**
- Listen quietly and supportively for 2–5 minutes without speaking yourself and without replying.
- Nod, smile and make appropriate 'Ahh', 'Mmm', 'Aha' noises and the like – but no words.
- Resist the urge to fill silences – just wait until they continue to speak (obviously, be sensitive and don't continue with the silence if they are becoming uncomfortable with it).

| | |
|---|---|
| | • Just listen to what they are saying, without making judgements, without making comparisons to your own experiences and without planning a reply. |
| 2 | **Notice how they respond to your undivided attention.**<br>If appropriate, you might ask them what it was like for them. |
| 3 | **Then consider:**<br>• When you listen to somebody with your full attention, like that, it's like what?<br>• What key differences do you notice between this kind of listening and your everyday kind of listening? |
| 4 | **The next time someone is listening to you without interrupting, notice what is it like for you.** (You might like to arrange for someone to listen to you like this, to ensure you experience it.) |
| 5 | **Then consider:**<br>• When someone listens to you with their full attention, like that, it's like what?<br>• What key differences do you notice between being listened to like this and being listened to in an everyday kind of way? |
| 6 | **Pay attention to the listening going on around you and identify examples of effective listening.** As well as everyday conversations, you could observe TV interviews and reflect on the effectiveness of the interviewers' listening styles. |
| | You may find it useful to draw/write your responses because later you will be modelling what you are like when you are listening at your best. |

---

### Task for week 2

- Use the opportunities presented to you this week to listen to someone with focused attention at least three times.
- Continue to use '... and what kind of (...)?' and listen with focused attention to the replies.

---

---

### Practice tips

- Whenever you find yourself in a conversation and someone is busy telling you something, clear your mind and focus (as you did in the activities above) for as long as it remains comfortable for the speaker.
- Practise with a range of different speakers.
- Be aware that while most people appreciate a good listener, some find it exposing and uncomfortable, so be sensitive to their response and act accordingly.
- Notice the responses to your listening.

---

# Week 3

## Is there anything else about questions?

The next question to introduce to your practice is, '... *and is there anything else?'* When you use this question, you (and the children) will find out more – more information and more detail. You may be surprised how much more you can tap into with the use of this one simple question. If you give them plenty of take-up time, children will search their minds for relevant information – and when they take the time to seek it, they will more often than not find it.

Of course, they could simply say 'no' and this does happen sometimes, either because there is nothing else to find, in which case you can move on in the conversation, or because the child is not engaging with the question – but even then, wait awhile and another answer will often come (you can see an example of this on page 52, where the child answers 'dunno'). The way to maximise engagement with the question is to ask with genuine curiosity, then wait and listen expectantly. The quality of your listening and attention has a direct effect on levels of engagement with the questions.

## Practice tips

- Even after a child has said 'no', wait awhile. Often 'no' is just the initial response and a few moments later another answer will come (see example on page 52). This is particularly the case if the child thinks they must have an instant answer and are not used to thinking more deeply.

- The quality of your waiting is significant. Wait with warmth, patience and expectancy.

You can ask this question again and again, after just about anything that is said. But because it's so useful and easy to tag on to anything, just keep a check, like you did with the first question, that you don't go so far as to cause a child to feel under pressure. On the other hand, don't be shy of asking it either – just be sensitive to reactions and stop if you notice any signs of discomfort.

This question helps the child to realise that there is a breadth to their thinking and knowledge, that there is rarely only one answer to a question and that they can be much more creative than they might have supposed.

| | |
|---|---|
| **Example (aged 11)** <br> *Continued from page 35.* | |
| Answer | Well, we're writing stories – it's all planned out – but I'm focusing on using paragraphs now, and linking them with pronouns and connectives like 'although', 'on the other hand' and 'meanwhile' … that kind of thing. |
| Question | Ah … and paragraphs and pronouns and connectives … <br> … and is there anything else? |
| Answer | Well, I'm going to use different length sentences, so some of them will have commas in them, for clauses. I've got to use adjectives, adverbs and adverbial phrases as well so it's interesting … and I'm going to get it all down in a first draft, then I'm going to play with the word order to make it better. I want it to be mysterious. |

Here are four forms of the question that you might like to try …

1.   … and is there anything else?

2.   … and is there anything else about that?

3.   … and is there anything else about (their exact words)?

4.   … and is there anything else about that (their exact word)?

Here are examples of the four different forms in action. The illustrations show the different kind of information elicited by each form of the question.

| Example 1 | | |
|---|---|---|
| Statement | It was a dog with orange and white fur and smooth, sharp white teeth and a long fluffy tail. And it jumped and played and panted. | |
| Question | ... and is there anything else? | |
| Answer | There were chickens there as well. | |
| **Example 2** | | |
| Statement | It was a dog with orange and white fur and smooth, sharp white teeth and a long fluffy tail. And it jumped and played and panted. | |
| Question | ... and is there anything else about that? | |
| Answer | Yes, the dog barked every time it jumped. | |
| **Example 3** | | |
| Statement | It was a dog with orange and white fur and smooth, sharp white teeth and a long fluffy tail. And it jumped and played and panted. | |
| Question | ... and is there anything else about *orange*? | |
| Answer | It is a warm colour – the colour of the setting sun. I like it – it makes me feel cosy. | |
| **Example 4** | | |
| Statement | It was a dog with orange and white fur and smooth, sharp white teeth and a long fluffy tail. And it jumped and played and panted. | |

| Question | ... and is there anything else about *that orange*? | |
|---|---|---|
| Answer | It was the exact same orangey brown colour as a fox. It made the dog look exactly like a fox. No wonder the chickens looked worried! | |

## Task for week 3

- Continue to ask '... and what kind of (...)?'

- Continue to listen with a focused awareness.

- Experiment with the '... and is there anything else?' questions, using the four different forms.

- Notice:

  > How much more information is elicited.

  > The different kinds of information elicited with the different forms of the question.

  > The contexts in which the different forms do and don't fit.

## Practice tip

These questions can stimulate a lot of thinking. Bear this in mind when you are asking them and direct your questions towards things that will be useful and comfortable to think about.

# Week 4

## Is there anything else about listening?

As you have been practising your listening skills, I imagine you will have noticed that people are telling you a whole lot more now – and you've had plenty of opportunity to use the clean questions. Now you can develop your listening skills further and practise focusing your attention with greater mastery.

First rid yourself of 'mental clutter'. Mental clutter may consist of thoughts and feelings generated during the day, burning issues which are currently on your mind, personal beliefs and prior assumptions and experiences. The problem with this kind of mental clutter is it can result in you having distorted perceptions and interpretations of the messages you are hearing.

> During a particularly lengthy writing session, a child asked if she could pop outside to breathe some fresh air and get some inspiration. I imagined she might be trying to avoid the work but I gave her the benefit of the doubt. Immediately, two of her best friends came to me and whispered sweetly, 'Please may we go outside to get some inspiration too?' I wanted to demonstrate trust in them, to encourage some self-responsibility, and so I said yes, despite a nagging feeling that they might be up to no good.
>
> After a short while I slipped outside to catch them red-handed but instead found them with their eyes closed, faces skyward, quietly crafting their compositions and whispering them to the clouds. As they finished they skipped back to their desks to resume their writing. I had totally misjudged them.

I'm certain that you have experienced occasions where you have made seemingly reasonable assumptions that turned out to be totally or partially inaccurate. It happens a lot. So how can you clear your mind of mental clutter, ready for listening? Here are a few ways other people have found helpful:

- Meditating.

- Writing thoughts down so they are not playing on your mind.

- Listing tasks or putting them in a diary so you don't have to remember them.

- Saying what is bugging you out loud (shouting it even!) and then letting it go.

- Letting less in (e.g. by limiting time spent on surfing the web, reading papers, watching TV) – the constant quest to keep informed and updated can be overwhelming.

- Using a mental activity like having a wind blow it all out of your mind or putting it in a drawer marked 'deal with later'.

From time to time, most people experience a kind of mental stillness in which they are fully open to listen. The next activity asks you to identify and model your own resourceful stillness. In preparation for the activity you might like to settle yourself comfortably where you can just relax undisturbed and be still for a while.

---

## Listening space

Now … recall a time in your life when you have been still and open …

As you remember, get a real-time sense of what it's like for you. Notice, for instance, what you are seeing, what you are hearing, what you are feeling, what you are tasting and what you are smelling.

… and when you are ready, take a moment and notice … *when you are like that … you are like what?* For example, are you like an empty vessel … a smooth ocean … the vast silence of empty space … or something else? … *you are like what?*

Draw or write a description (or both) of what you are like when you are still and open like that.

Remember: Now that you know what you are like when you are open to listening, you can use this resourceful metaphor whenever you want to listen well – by recalling it and by experiencing it in real time with all your

---

senses, just as you did in the previous exercise.

The next time you find yourself in a situation when you need to listen effectively, remember to use it: recall what you are like and step into it, put it on, remind yourself of it or in some other way embrace it – whatever works well for you.

When you have cleared your mind ready for listening, you can start to engage with more than just your ears. Begin to listen with your ears, your eyes and your feeling sense. Listen with total focus to what is said, how it is said and the body language employed (e.g. gestures, posture, facial expression, direction of gaze).

When you begin to listen with all your senses, you will be paying attention to subtle messages *within* the message. These can show themselves through, for example, tone or cadence of voice, choice of words, signs of emotion or changes in energy and in what is said as well as in what is not said – in what is left out.

Beyond this, you can listen with a global focus – sensing the atmosphere around and between, being fully present and connecting with intuition. This level of listening is rarely used or even recognised in everyday life. It can take time and practice to experience and become familiar with this listening state, so there is no need to rush. As you practise listening you will become increasingly sensitive to these kinds of cues, so allow it to happen at your own pace and in your own way.

At the point of listening, hold in mind that:

- Your experience is not their experience and vice versa – even if it seems to be the same on the face of it.

- Even if it seems that you know what they are talking about, you can only know to a limited degree.

And let that sit well with you. When you become comfortable with not knowing and can enjoy the journey as information unfolds before you (rather than trying to second guess the destination), you will be listening non-judgementally. And with Clean Language the primary purpose of listening is to support the *speaker*. Eliciting information is a by-product of that listening rather than its aim.

A natural consequence of listening in this way is an increase in respect. Bryant McGill (2012: 5) remarks that 'one of the most sincere forms of respect is actually listening to what another has to say'. Be aware that as you tune in to the speaker with a genuine, open, curious attitude, your respect for them will naturally grow, and you will be nurturing their respect for themselves – all of which creates conditions for the growth of self-respect and self-esteem.

## Task for week 4

Continue to practise using the clean questions and add in some exquisitely focused listening:

- Choose quiet times when there is minimal chance of interruption or distraction to listen to pupils, colleagues, friends and family.

- Then, when you feel confident (and with their agreement), use clean questions in conversations with individual children in the classroom.

- Respond to speakers by repeating back their exact words before delivering your question.

## Practice tips

Be patient with yourself – these skills will take some practice:

- You don't need to repeat back everything (especially if the speaker has said a lot), just key sentences, phrases or words. This lets the speaker know you have not only listened but also that you have heard exactly what they have said. One of the by-products of doing this is that children and adults come to realise that what they say means something and these are *their* words and thoughts and no one else's. They want to pay more attention to the words they use since someone is going to take what they say seriously.

- Relax, soft focus your eyes and take in the whole picture.

- As you challenge children with questions, hold in mind the entreaty by Yeats to 'Tread softly because you tread on my dreams'.

# Week 5

## ... and what would you like to have happen? (Part 1)

You have probably noticed how much easier it is for people to know what they don't like and what they don't want than what they do like and what they do want. When you ask children to suggest rules for the classroom, they often find it much easier to say what not to do than what to do.

Obviously, everyone is different but it does seem quite common for people to have a natural default setting biased towards knowing more about – and being much clearer about – what they don't like or don't want. Focusing on what you don't like/don't want can be a safe option because it doesn't commit you to anything – there's no call to action.

Of course, children are renowned for their talent of asking for what they want (they have a reputation for pester power), but when you observe a little more closely you will find they too often know less about, or less clearly, what they like or want than what they don't like or don't want. There is a problem with this as a default way of thinking: unless you are clear about what you do like or want, how can you achieve it or bring it about?

## Task for week 5

- Continue to practise using the two clean questions you have learned so far, along with exquisitely focused listening.

- Subtly and respectfully tune in to some of the conversations you hear around you – picking out any expressions of liking or wanting and any expressions of not liking or not wanting.

- Because you will be observing and not joining in the conversations, you will be getting a chance to hone your listening skills at the same time.

- Don't make any judgements about what you are hearing – just notice whether it's a like/want statement or a don't like/don't want statement. (Moaning is usually a don't like/don't want statement, as are complaining and blaming.)

- You might like to record the number of like/want and don't like/don't want statements you witness and build a picture of their relative frequencies. Most people log a far greater proportion of don't like/don't want statements than like/want ones.

In short, people often know what they don't want – they have it right there at their fingertips, often in rich detail. But if individuals know clearly what they do want, they are more likely to be able to move towards it or bring it about (there is more on this in Chapter 6).

You have begun to practise a way of listening and questioning that can help people to gain clearer and more detailed understandings of their thoughts and feelings, so how can you use it to help children and colleagues (and yourself) to develop rich, detailed ideas of what they want? This is where the next clean question comes into play.

# Week 6

## ... and what would you like to have happen? (Part 2)

When you hear a child or a colleague (or yourself) complaining about something they don't want, if they are happy for you to intervene, repeat their words back to them and continue with '... and what would you like to have happen?'

Lunchtime supervisors were tired of the rowdy behaviour during the line-up time at the end of lunch break. They complained that the children did not stop playing as soon as the whistle had blown, that individual children would regularly lag behind or not line up at all and that children did not stand quietly or still in the line. Conversations in relation to this unwanted behaviour became commonplace but the behaviour continued.

Then one of them asked '… and what would you *like* to have happen?' and the dynamics changed. They began to detail the kinds of behaviour they wanted to see. They then started to notice that the majority of the children were indeed doing what was wanted. They began to think of strategies to motivate those who were not doing what was wanted or to remove them from the playground before the whistle was blown. Line-up times became a much more peaceful and positive experience for everyone.

Notice how the question shifted their focus from the problem towards a desired outcome – it flipped their thinking.

Children (and adults) may find it difficult to respond straight away, so be patient while they are thinking and, if necessary, repeat the question. The time required for thinking is often much longer than you might be used to giving – much more than 'good practice' generally dictates. So become comfortable with periods of silence and wait patiently with an affirmative, expectant and curious attitude, as this will support their thinking.

Many people find that giving sufficient time is surprisingly challenging and they are tempted to 'help' the person who is thinking by offering ideas or options – especially when that person is a child. This may speed up the process but it will stop the thinking in its tracks. Instead, cultivate levels of patience and trust that will allow you to give them all the time they need.

Thinking about what they want can be quite unfamiliar to some people. Some individuals are so unused to thinking in terms of outcomes (what they would like) that they may need time, practice and a little coaching in order to answer this question at all. My experience, though, is that children tend to take to it like ducks to water and those children who are less used to thinking in terms of outcomes adapt to it pretty quickly as well.

---

### Task for week 6

- Listen for problem statements and use '... and what would you like to have happen?' to refocus the thinking on to an outcome.

- When the reply comes, assuming it's a desired outcome and not another problem, you can help them to consider and develop it in more detail by asking the clean questions you have already practised (and are probably well-acquainted with by now): '... and what kind of (...)?' and '... and is there anything else about (...)?'

---

And depending on what they are speaking/thinking about, you may choose to use ...

# Week 7

## ... and where/whereabouts is (...)?

This question will help recipients become more aware of the location of their perception (the thing they are thinking about). You needn't confine the question to objects – you can ask about feelings and ideas as well.

| Example 1 | | |
|---|---|---|
| Statement | This is my *candlestick* design. | |
| Question | ... and this is your candlestick design ... and what kind of *candlestick*? | |

| | | |
|---|---|---|
| Answer | It's a tall *candlestick* with *holly leaves*. | |
| Question | ... and a tall *candlestick* with holly leaves ... and is there anything else about *candlestick*? | |
| Answer | It has a hole in the top for the candle. | |
| Question | ... and a hole in the top for the candle ... and tall ... and *holly leaves* ... and what kind of *holly leaves*? | |
| Answer | Quite flat with curled edges and blunt spikes, so they don't break or cut you – but I haven't drawn them. | |
| Question | ... and blunt spikes ... and curled edges ... and quite flat ... and holly leaves ... and where are those *holly leaves*? | |
| Answer | Well, there's a ring of them at the top to catch the wax when it runs down the candle, and there's a base of them at the bottom to make it stand up and catch any more wax if it runs over the top ones. | |
| **Example 2** | | |
| Statement | I feel *happy*. | |
| Question | ... and when you feel *happy*, whereabouts do you feel *happy*? | |

| Answer | Happy ... hmm ... happy here in my tummy. | |
|--------|-------------------------------------------|---|

**Example 3**

| Statement | I *get rid* of the 2 first – then add the 10 and the 20. | |
|-----------|--------------------------------------------------------|---|
| Question | ... and you *get rid* of the 2 first – then add the 10 and the 20 ... and when ... *get rid* of the 2 ... what kind of *get rid*? | |
| Answer | I dunno – I *shove it away* (*with a shoving gesture*). | |
| Question | ... and you *shove it away* ...<br>and when ... *shove it away* ... whereabouts *away*? | |
| Answer | Well, I get it off the 20, so it's not 22, it's 20 (because they're just units and the 20 is two 10's) ... and I shove it *out* until I've finished and then it can go back. | |
| Question | ... and you *shove it out* until you've finished ... and when ... *shove it out* ... whereabouts *out*? | |
| Answer | Oh, over here (*gestures to a spot in mid-air*). It's out the way of 20 ... I see it there, then I don't forget to put it back when I've done 10 plus 20. It's not right away so I can't see it – 'cos then I forget it. | |

## Task for week 7

- Practise using all four questions to help develop rich detail about what they want (this is called 'developing an outcome') and notice the results.

- Begin to notice the different contexts in your work and life where you can use your clean skills and log them (e.g. in the playground when children are bored or in conflict with others, in lessons to enhance assessment for learning, for thinking through problems, to support your planning or for behaviour management).

  > When might you use clean skills?

  > What will you use clean skills for?

  > Who will you use clean skills with?

  > Why will you use clean skills?

  > What will it be like for you?

  > What will it be like for the children?

- Expand on these ideas – bring them to life and make them tangible:

  > Develop a vision of your next steps by asking yourself a few clean questions.

  > Start by asking, 'What would you like to have happen?' Note your responses.

  > Go on to develop rich detail by asking the other three questions about the various aspects of your response: 'And is there anything else about (...)?', 'And what kind of (...)?', 'And where/whereabouts is (...)?'

Remember: You can ask any question in any order and any of the questions as many times as is appropriate – you don't need to stop after four questions.

Although there are more clean questions for you to become familiar with, the four you have been practising will suffice for most situations to begin with. It's a good idea to integrate them into your everyday classroom practice before adding more.

# Chapter 3
# More About the Questions

Clean questions are clean, simple and repetitive. The small iterations, repeated over and over are what make the questions powerful.

**David Grove, 'Summary of David Grove's Ideas – As of 2003' (2003)**

Having integrated the first four questions into your everyday practice, you should find it relatively easy to begin to use some additional questions – and you will probably be able to accommodate them at a much faster pace now. In this chapter you will find more questions; information on the functions of the questions; how to ask them to direct attention – and you will begin to explore what to ask them of.

The questions have varied functions and can be categorised according to those functions. In a school context, I have found it useful to categorise them as *developing*, *sequence* and *intention* questions because it helps me to remember them (they are grouped according to their purpose); to select a suitable question when working 'in the moment'; to see how the questions work as a coherent method (to bring to light attributes, patterns, relationships and systems) – and to acknowledge the structure of experience.

## The three functions of Clean Language

Clean Language offers an excellent framework for gathering information, for modelling and for facilitating learning and change. Using the questions for gathering information is fairly straightforward and you will have already begun to do it if you have completed the practical tasks described earlier in this section.

There are various ways to group them, so after you have assessed my categorisations, I encourage you to develop a grouping that will work well for you.

# Developing questions

I refer to the following questions as developing questions. These questions freeze-frame thinking so that you and a child (or children) can examine it and become more keenly aware of its content.

- And is there anything else about (...)?

- And what kind of (...)?

- And where is (...)?

- And whereabouts is (...)?

- And is there a relationship between (...) and (...)?

- And that's (...) like what?

# Sequence questions

Sequence questions focus attention on the order of steps in a process, on a series of perceptions in time and space or on the origin (the source) of a perception. Whereas developing questions stop things in their tracks, these questions map out the action.

- And then what happens?

- And what happens next?

- And what happens just before?

- And what happens just after (...) and just before (...)?

- And what happens between (...) and (...)?

- And where does (...) come from?

- And where could (...) come from?

- And when (...), what happens to (...)?

# Intention questions

Intention questions focus attention on desired outcomes and the conditions necessary to achieve them.

- And what would you like to have happen?

- And what would (...) like to have happen?

- And what needs to happen for (...)?

- And is there anything else that needs to happen for (...)?

- And what determines whether (...)?

- And can (...)?

# How to ask Clean Language questions: the three-part syntax

The syntax of clean questions – the way words or phrases are arranged to make a sentence – is unusual. You will have noticed that some of the questions have incorrect grammar. This is not a mistake but it may take a bit of getting used to. With clean questions you need to repeat back words and phrases exactly as they have been spoken. This is known as parrot-phrasing (as opposed to paraphrasing, which reproduces the gist without using the exact words). I find it helps to think of a child's parrot-phrased words blended into a question as a complete and discrete 'symbol of meaning' – almost like a flash card.

When I blend this 'symbol' into the question I speak it as a single item. It helps me to think of it as a single item when I remember that I don't actually know what it means. The words may be familiar to me but the meaning resides with its owner. I've used brackets in the following table to contain these words. I think of the words between the brackets as a 'one-unit symbol' rather than a meaningful phrase or sentence, which I then blend into the question.

The three-part syntax of a clean question works to:

1. Acknowledge what the other person has said. It also gives that person an opportunity to hear and acknowledge for themselves what they have just said.

2. Direct their attention to a particular aspect of their thinking.

3. Set them off in pursuit of knowledge – to search for an answer.

# Focusing attention

Notice in the example below how the focus narrows from *a green grasshopper hopping on the grass* to *a grasshopper hopping* and then to *hopping*.

| | Syntax | How to ask the questions |
|---|---|---|
| 1 | … and (…) | … and (a green grasshopper hopping on the grass) |
| 2 | … and when/as (…) | … and when (a grasshopper hopping) |
| 3 | … clean question? | … what kind of (hopping) is that (hopping)? |

The three-part syntax is a way of training the child's attention incrementally on a discrete part of a perception:

1. First, you parrot-phrase the child's exact words, adding an 'and' to the beginning of the sentence.

2. Next, you isolate a phrase/part of the sentence, narrowing the focus, adding '… and when' to the beginning of the sentence (alternatively use '… and as' if you are referring to something that is happening in the moment or to a process, action or event that happens over a period of time).

3. For the final part of the syntax you can narrow the focus still further, isolating a particular word (or element) to blend into a clean question.

The first, second and third parts of the syntax help to train the child's attention, step by step, on to the element you have selected. This helps them to keep track and understand and to focus on the particular element, and it provides time (and scaffolding) for their thinking as they do so.

As children become familiar with this style of questioning, and begin to adopt the framework to guide their own thinking, they become more discriminating, focused and systematic in their thinking.

## Practice tips

- Using the three-part syntax to deliver clean questions is effective in encouraging breadth and depth of thinking. It may seem clumsy to you (especially at first when you are new to using it) but rarely to the person being questioned because they will respond by thinking deeply about what they have been asked.

- Bear in mind that having learned to use it you are not tied to using it every time, as you can see from some of the examples in this book. It's worthwhile developing the capability to switch between the three-part syntax and a shorter, more conversational approach (which you have been using thus far) so that you are able to respond flexibly according to the context.

# Words in the spotlight

In the example of the green grasshopper hopping above, the attention was directed to the word *hopping* – a verb. For most people, nouns – especially long ones (ones with the most letters) – are the most obvious words to focus on in a sentence, but verbs, though often overlooked, can be especially interesting words to explore.

Be aware that you can ask about any or all of the words in a sentence. Your selection will depend on the purpose you have in asking. In the example of the green grasshopper hopping on the grass, for instance, you might like to ask:

- … and a green grasshopper hopping on the grass … and is there anything else about *a* … when *a* green grasshopper?

- … and a green grasshopper hopping on the grass … and when a green grasshopper … what kind of green is that *green*?

- … and a green grasshopper hopping on the grass … and when grasshopper hopping … is there a relationship between *grasshopper* and *grass*?

- … and a green grasshopper hopping on the grass … and when hopping on the grass … is there anything else about *on* … when hopping *on* the grass?

- … and a green grasshopper hopping on the grass … and when on the grass … is there anything else about *the* … when hopping on *the* grass?

- … and a green grasshopper hopping on the grass … and when hopping on the grass … what kind of *grass* is that *grass*?

As you explore asking the questions, notice the effects of asking about words you wouldn't usually ask about – for instance, prepositions:

- … and is there anything else about *in*?

- … and what kind of *in*?

- … and what kind of *through*?

- … and whereabouts, *through*?

(We'll look at these effects more closely in Chapter 4 on metaphors.)

---

## Practice task

- Practise formulating and asking clean questions using the three-part syntax.

- Practise formulating and asking clean questions using the three-part syntax with your class.

- Notice how the syntax leads the children's attention steadily to a point of focus.

- Explore the three-part syntax, asking about words you wouldn't usually choose to explore. You might like to write down the speaker's first sentence and then go through the sentence, one word at a time, asking clean questions (using the three-part syntax) of each word in turn.

- Log what you notice.

---

## Practice tip

As you experiment, be aware that some questions will fall flat – the child may not have a clue what you mean. When this happens, it's not a problem; just move on and ask a different question. As you become more experienced about what to put in the spotlight this will happen less often, but it can happen to even the most experienced facilitator.

# Chapter 4
# Metaphor

Metaphorical thought is unavoidable, ubiquitous, and mostly unconscious.

George Lakoff and Mark Johnson, *Metaphors We Live By* (1980)

The root of the word 'metaphor' is the Greek and Latin word *metaphora*, meaning to transfer or to carry across. The efficacy of metaphors lies in their capacity to communicate large volumes of information (sometimes highly complex) in a single chunk.

In the introduction, we saw how David Grove recognised the significance of metaphor for communication and meaning-making, both interpersonal and intrapersonal. Chapter 3 focused attention on individual words in sentences and, if you have practised asking clean questions of the less obvious words (see page 60), you will have experienced the (sometimes surprisingly) vast range of meanings they hold. This chapter builds on that knowledge and experience to explore the role of explicit and implicit metaphors in learning and change, and provides examples of how learning metaphors can be developed in the classroom.

## Metaphors and the way we live

If you think life has a pecking order, you will probably aim to find your place within it – perhaps fighting your way to the top, staying compliantly at the bottom or defending your position in the middle. If you see life as a team game you will play your role and may aim to fit in with others for the sake of a good team performance. If you think life is about the survival of the fittest you will behave accordingly. And if you think we are all connected as one you will behave differently again.

Metaphors can be considered as being of two main types: implicit and explicit.

# Explicit metaphors

Explicit metaphors state the characteristic being compared (e.g. he was as strong as an ox, the house was so cold – it was a fridge). When you examine the language your pupils are using you will find they use explicit metaphors frequently. Teachers often use metaphors to help children understand new things and to make complex ideas simple, so when you examine your own sentences you will find plenty of examples too. Explicit metaphors are said to appear in our speech at a rate of approximately six per minute (see Tosey et al., 2013).

# Implicit metaphors

Implicit metaphors are those which imply meaning and/or comparison rather than stating it directly (e.g. he was an ox of a man, the house was a fridge). Many implicit metaphors operate outside of awareness. When you examine the language your pupils are using you will find they are steeped in implicit metaphors, which influence their thinking – albeit imperceptibly.

Most of us, most of the time, are influenced by metaphors outside of our awareness. (For example, we may or may not believe that Coke is the 'real thing' but tend to concede, without question, that the real thing is something desirable and that attaining the real thing is worthwhile – the 'real thing' part of the metaphor slips in under the radar.) When we become aware of them we're less likely to be at their mercy.

Sometimes, when metaphors (like the 'real thing') are subject to scrutiny, they change – awareness itself is enough to initiate a change. Metaphors don't need to be changed, change just happens. That's learning.

# How do you become aware of implicit metaphors?

The words we use can be clues to the implicit metaphors we're using. Language is peppered with prepositions, which are used to communicate both literal and metaphorical meanings.

The cat sat *on* the mat.

The cat's attention was *on* the mouse.

You can often tell if a preposition is being used metaphorically by asking yourself, 'Is this possible (or happening) in the physical world?' I've listed a few examples in the table below, and I'm sure you can call to mind many of your own.

| Prepositions | |
|---|---|
| **Literal** | **Metaphorical** |
| The water is *in* the cup. | I am *in* a bad mood. |
| She jumped *over* the fence. | I'm getting *over* a cold. |
| He crawled *under* the table. | I've been feeling *under* the weather. |

| | |
|---|---|
| The thread is passed *through* the eye of the needle. | I've been going *through* a bit of a bad patch. |
| She's hiding *behind* the wall. | Now I'm *behind* with my work. |
| He's working *outside* the classroom. | I'm *outside* my comfort zone. |

Not all examples fit so neatly though. Sometimes a word can be used in both literal and metaphoric ways. Take for example the phrase 'he leaned on her'. The 'on' may be used to denote being physically on her or to denote being metaphorically on her. Whether a word is used in a literal or a metaphoric way depends on the context. So another useful way to help decide if a word is being used metaphorically is whether you can say, 'It's as if … ', 'It's like … ' or 'It's as though … ', and the sentence still makes sense. 'It's as if he leaned on her', 'It's like he leaned on her', 'It's as though he leaned on her' only make sense if the 'on' is used metaphorically.

Verbs are often used metaphorically too.

## Verbs

| Literal | Metaphorical |
|---|---|
| *Sailing* the boat. | *Sailing* through the exams. |
| *Skipping* in the playground. | *Skipping* lunch. |
| She *pushed* me over. | She *pushed* the boundaries. |
| He *pulled* my hair. | He *pulled* the wool over my eyes. |
| *Jumping* in PE. | *Jumping* to conclusions. |
| *Grasping* the crayon. | *Grasping* the concept. |

Again you need to use discernment in order to decide if a verb is being used literally or metaphorically. In 'he leaned on her', the word 'leaned' might refer either to the physical action (i.e. to incline at an angle, which in combination with the words 'on her' suggest an element of physical pressure at the point of contact with her) or to a metaphorical one (i.e. to apply mental pressure – to press her into action or, conversely, to be dependent or reliant on her).

# Metaphors in the classroom

Most of the time, using words in a metaphorical way is helpful because it offers a means to convey meaning efficiently. But sometimes the implications of an implicit metaphor can be unresourceful, and this is where Clean Language can usefully direct attention and raise awareness – making the implicit explicit.

The classroom is a common context for unresourceful metaphors. Take 'trying hard' for instance. Children often think (and are told) that the key to success is 'trying hard'. What kind of trying? What kind of hard? When examined using Clean Language, it's clear that for many children 'trying hard' is counterproductive.

Children's metaphors for 'trying hard' which I've elicited using Clean Language include, 'A kind of hard ball in my stomach', 'My eyes like lasers burning' and 'Pushing myself, like a snow plough'. Their accompanying gestures include tight fists, tension in the neck, holding the breath, clenched teeth, stiff limbs and grimacing. When children become aware of the states they are creating in themselves as they begin to 'try hard' (or think of 'trying hard'), they are often moved to reconsider what will assist them to perform at their best, knowing that those negative physical states can impede high-level performance.

Children are often amused as they realise how obstructive their 'trying hard' has been, and go on to explore what they need to be like to perform at their best (see page 73, 'Developing a learning metaphor for the classroom') – for example, 'the sun shining on', 'a butterfly', 'superman with a cape', 'a motocross rider' or 'a spaceship'. When children discover what they are like when they are learning at their best, motivation goes through the roof.

Some perspectives on learning appear to be more resourceful than others in terms of attainment in schools. Carol Dweck (2007) found that the beliefs and associated assumptions that students hold about learning and success affect their outcomes. According to her study, the growth metaphor is clearly an effective one for success in school.

---

## Practice task

- Begin to get a sense of some of the *implicit metaphors* children are using in class:

  > Lightly and gently question a couple of them.

  > Reflect: What might be the implications of these metaphors?

- Aim to get a sense of children's *learning metaphors* (see pages 73–101):

  > Lightly and gently question a couple of them.

  > Reflect: What might be the implications of these metaphors?

  > How might this impact your planning?

- Explore your own metaphors – for example:

  > Life ... life is like what?

  > Teaching ... teaching is like what?

  > Learning ... learning is like what?

  > (A prevailing social metaphor of your choice) ... is like what?

Ask clean questions to develop a sense of these metaphors.

---

# When metaphors change

In the early days of my career I would find the summer terms particularly tiring and would, more often than not, begin the summer holidays exhausted and in need of recuperation. It's a fairly common experience among teachers. In school we would start each summer term with a planning meeting, during which we would talk about the approaching term using the metaphor of being on a roller coaster. It started at a hair-raising pace, only to accelerate and become more and more nerve-wracking as we hurtled towards the end.

We created a monster of a metaphor, which served as a self-inflicted stressor, and never stopped to question its validity because it fitted our experience like a glove. We tightened our grip, clenched our teeth and prepared to hang on in there. It's so easy to embody metaphors like this and be unaware of the pervasive effect they are having on you. That tension can spread throughout your body and then beyond into your social setting, affecting the people around you until it's a part of the system. It's embedded – it's just the way it *is* around here.

When I realised what had been happening surreptitiously below my level of awareness, the spell was broken. I knew I didn't want the roller coaster approach any more. Once I had seen the metaphor for what it was, I couldn't take it seriously. It seemed ludicrous. Why on earth would I *choose* to feel this kind of tension and terror for three long months? How could it possibly support anyone to perform at their best?

I began to see the summer term as a time of sunshine and laughter, activity and growth. It was like bobbing along in a rowing boat enjoying the sights and the sounds of a meandering river. As work tasks floated towards me I would reach out, lift them into the boat and deal with them. This felt so much better than before, when I had been hurtling along a track towards them, heart in mouth.

With this new metaphor my body felt relaxed and I moved differently. My walk had more of a saunter as though I were on holiday. I had a sense that 'to everything there is a season, and a time for every purpose'. The tasks still had to be done, and to the same timescales, but deadlines lost their terror. Even when many tasks came floating along together and it was a challenge to gather them all up, pull them into the boat and deal with them, it was an enjoyable challenge (I suppose fishermen know this) – exhilarating.

Nowadays, I have a sense of making hay while the sun shines and a delight in the culmination of a year's work – enjoying and witnessing the children blossom and grow. Tiredness is a different kind of tiredness; it's the satisfying 'phew' at the end of a glorious day tending the garden. It's a 'time for a well-deserved cuppa' kind of feeling – invigorating.

Now I know the exhaustion I had experienced previously was created by hanging on tightly to the roller coaster tension I had been generating for months at a time through my own thinking. As soon as I became aware of it, and could replace it with a metaphor I liked, my thinking lost its hold on me – and everything changed for the better.

## How do your implicit metaphors affect your experiences?

Thinking about your own context and your working practices ...

- Your working practices are like what?

It sometimes helps to draw or write your description.

- And when your working practices are like that ... what happens to ... your body, your emotions, your behaviour, the people around you?

- And knowing that ... what would you like to have happen now?

It sometimes helps to draw or write your description.

Just as we can create stress in ourselves through our own thinking, so the children in your class can experience stress as a result of their thinking. You have no doubt come across children who experience nerves in the lead-up to exams or tests. Some suffer such extreme stress that their ability to perform is seriously impeded. Likewise, children can build resistance towards (or fear of) writing, maths, PE, drawing – all kinds of activities – through their thinking. But if children become aware of their thinking, it can lose its grip on them too. You can support their raised awareness by considering their underlying metaphors and how they impact on their working practices.

## How do children's implicit metaphors affect their experiences?

Thinking about the children in their classroom context and their working practices ...

• Their working practices are like what?

It sometimes helps to draw or write your description.

• And when their working practices are like that ... what happens to ... their bodies, their emotions, their behaviour, the people around them?

• And knowing that ... what would you like to have happen now?

It sometimes helps to draw or write your description.

Given that metaphor underpins our understanding of the world and the way we interact with it, when metaphors change then understandings, perspectives and ways of being change along with them. No doubt you will recall an earlier example of this from the introduction – the student teacher's image of the little boy transforming into a large gremlin overnight. You may also have noticed shifts occurring in your own metaphors. What changes have you noticed? What are the effects of those changes?

A metaphor landscape can change in multitudes of ways. Here are a few examples:

- The form of a symbol may change – for example, a symbol may become larger or smaller, a different colour or texture, or a completely different object (a cup may change to a saucer).

- The position of a symbol may change – for example, a symbol may move nearer or further away, higher or lower, to the right or the left, clockwise or anticlockwise, or turn around in another plane.

- The relationships between symbols may change – for example, changes may occur in the distance between them, their size in relation to others, their position in relation to others, their attitude/intentions towards others.

Note: The word 'symbol' is used here to denote the individual components which make up a metaphor. A system of symbols is known as a 'metaphor landscape' and denotes the structure of a metaphor, the system of symbols it contains, the arrangement of the symbols and the relationships between them.

This is not an exhaustive list. As you work with your pupils, you will probably notice other categories of change. Sometimes changes can be fairly major and obvious and sometimes they are subtler or seemingly insignificant.

The magnitude of a change in a metaphor landscape doesn't necessarily have a direct relationship with the magnitude of change in perspective and meaning. Notice how changes in the following images give rise to changes in your own perspective.

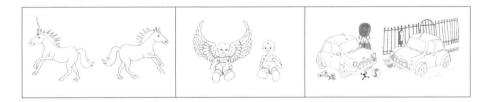

Changes in metaphors are indicative of changes in thinking, which are often evidenced by changes in perspective and/or behaviour. When modelling cleanly, your role is to notice and ask about the changes, *not to interpret or make assumptions* about the meanings of such changes and *not to try to bring about change.*

It's about helping someone to become aware of their metaphors (and of any changes that arise in their metaphors) without imparting any judgement or directive influence.

When working in this way, as a teacher, I've noticed my biggest challenges have been to:

- Let go of the need to control.

- Give up on thinking that I know best – or that I need to know best.

- Give up thinking I need to know the outcome in advance.

- Give adequate time.

- Trust.

It's been about adopting a 'horse whispering' approach rather than a 'horse breaking' one. This change in perspective affects my relationship to the way children learn and thereby affects all that I do.

---

## Practice task

- Notice the words you use when you talk about *facilitating learning*.

- Notice the words you use when you talk about *teaching*.

- List them in separate columns.

- Note the differences between them.

- Recall common metaphors for learning (page 14):

  > What is your metaphor for facilitating learning? What are the implications for this metaphor?

  > What is your metaphor for teaching? What are the implications for this metaphor?

Note: You may be interested to consider the influence that our language has over the metaphors we adopt and the implications. It's difficult for English speakers to talk about *communication* in terms other than a 'conduit metaphor'. Sometimes

---

teaching has been (and is) thought of in these terms – teachers package information (content) and deliver it to children to be received and assimilated as is without question. (For more on the conduit metaphor see Reddy, 1993.)

Of course, changes in metaphor landscapes, in perspectives or in behaviour are all indicators that learning has happened because learning involves change.

## Developing a learning metaphor for the classroom

It's worthwhile taking the time to develop 'learning at my best' metaphors with the children in your class at the beginning of each year to establish constructive ways of working right from the start, because you will reap the benefits throughout the year. It's a wonderfully positive way for children to become engaged in and take ownership of the everyday working practices in the classroom by developing conditions that support their own learning needs and those of their peers.

I experienced the value of modelling 'learning at my best' first hand as an introductory activity on Wendy Sullivan and Judy Rees' Clean Summer School in Cambridge in 2007. The work is based on an idea originally developed by Caitlin Walker for use by pupils outside the mainstream school system. It enables learners to know what they need for their best learning to happen and it puts learners in the driving seat. In 2006, Walker taught lecturers at Liverpool John Moores University to use this technique with students during tutorials. They helped one another to develop models for learning at their best, keeping time and making good decisions. Their results increased from 49% achieving first and second class honours to over 73%, and this has remained consistent to date.

# When I'm learning at my best, I'm like what?

## Familiarisation activities

During the first few weeks of term, familiarisation activities help children to be prepared for considering what they are like when they are learning at their best (see Chapter 7). And when the children are confident enough with the questions, we all embark on the learning at my best activity together.[1] By 'confident enough' I mean the children are familiar with the questions and how they are used, with sensing and talking about what it's like for them when they are learning at their best and comfortable and practised with imagining.

This is also a good time to familiarise teaching assistants and other adults with the approach and the expectations (see below), because they will need to be prepared to share their insights openly with the children if they are going to assist most effectively. This might be unfamiliar territory for some. They may need time and a little practical experience before they are happy to join in with authenticity. When you are aiming to work cleanly, faking it won't make it.

## First-hand experience for assistants

Because it's so valuable for assistants to experience the process and to be comfortable about engaging wholeheartedly, it's useful to make time for them to experience it first hand, prior to helping with a whole-class activity. Finding the time to facilitate assistants can be challenging but it's well worth the effort. Once, when I couldn't find any time for it during the day, I facilitated a teaching assistant on the telephone during the evening, and even though this meant her giving up 30 minutes of her precious home life, she still values the experience and the benefits she gained from it, even years later.

---

1   It's perfectly possible to do the activity with one small group at a time, but you will need to plan for everyone to share their insights with the rest of the class in a whole-class plenary.

# Whole-class demonstration

After the familiarisation period, and with the help of an assistant (an experienced adult or child), I demonstrate the learning at my best activity so that everyone has a good idea of what to expect and a chance to ask any questions.

Here's a transcript of a demonstration with a teaching assistant:

Me: And when you were learning at your best ... that's like what?

Andie: When I'm learning, and I'm learning new things and I'm really pleased to learn what I didn't know before, I feel like a pressure in my chest ... and it's like a hot-water bottle ... that spreads in my chest. And it makes me feel really proud because perhaps it's been really difficult and I've carried on ... because I've really wanted to know how to do something. Or I've learned ... and it's like big pressure in my chest ... but it's a nice pressure.

Me: Mmm ... a pressure ... and ... in your chest ... whereabouts in your chest?

Andie: It starts here and it goes down to where my heart is (*places hand on chest*) and it makes me feel, almost like my heart's swelling up ... because I'm really feeling ... it's not a horrible feeling ... it's a really, really nice feeling ... that's almost being ... full up.

Me: Oh ... a nice feeling ... almost being full up ... and goes there (*gesturing to the place where her hand is resting, on her chest*) and down to your heart ... and it spreads.

Andie: Yeah, it spreads and it's a lovely warm feeling.

Me: ... and is there anything else about that?

Andie: Err ... I might feel a bit tingly ... a little bit like, err ... stardust feeling!

Me: Oh ... stardust feeling ... and whereabouts stardust feeling?

Andie: Oh ... in my head.

Me: Oh ... in your head?

Andie: Like I feel my brain's working.

Me: Yeah? Is that inside or outside?

Andie:   Yes, inside ... a little bit of stardust going on.

Me:      ... and does it have a size or a shape?

Andie:   Very small ... little bits ... clashing together to make big bits ... a bit like fireworks going off ... you have a little bit ... and then a *big* ... big show.

Me:      Ah ... and so pressure ... that goes to your heart ... and spreads ... and little bits ...

Andie:   Yes! ... Tiny bits that bang together ... bang together to make big bits ... keep, keep going.

Me:      ... and is there anything else ... when you are learning at your best like that ... is there anything else?

Andie:   Lots of colours. Not flat colours ... lots of nice colours ... pale blues and pinks ... just nice things that make me feel relaxed ... and ... I like it to be nice and quiet ... not silent ... but nice and quiet.

Me:      ... and when quiet ... whereabouts quiet?

Andie:   Nice and quiet inside ... especially if I'm finding something hard ... just quietly sit still for a minute to prepare myself.

Me:      ... and whereabouts inside?

Andie:   In my stomach ... sometimes, when something's hard ... and you can get fed up with doing it ... in my stomach ... and relax that.

Me:      ... and that quiet is in your stomach?

Andie:   Yeah ... just here ... just here ... yeah ... yeah ...

Me:      ... and does that have a size or a shape?

Andie:   It's about sort of as big as my fist ... sometimes it feels ... if things get a bit ... it's a bit churny and a bit turned ... it sort of feels like it's twisting ... then I sort of think quietly ... think quiet thoughts ... and it just *stills* just to a ... the same, same, same, same size ... but instead of doing all this ... it just ... it *stills*.

Me:      Wow ... and it just *stills* ... and ... take all the time you need to think about all of that ... and draw all of that. And sometimes people may notice more as they're drawing ... and get that down too.

# Whole-class facilitation

After the demonstration, I lead the process with the whole group – adults and children. When everyone joins in like this, it reinforces that we're all learners and we all have needs which need to be met if we're to learn/teach/be at our best in our classroom environment.

Everyone finds a place where they would like to be – most are comfortable at their desks, some choose to rest their heads on their arms and some choose to lie on the floor. I check that everyone can remember a time when they were learning at their best (they will have had experiences of this as part of the preparation – see Chapter 7).

I talk them through a multisensory visualisation and they recall a time when they are doing something they have learned to do well. I speak slowly … and with pauses … to allow the children time … to … imagine … at every stage.

This is the kind of thing I say:

> Remember a time when you were learning something new … it's going well … and you are learning easily. Close your eyes and imagine you are there now.
>
> Notice what's happening … (*children share examples: learning a dance, to ride a bike, to play a guitar, to paint a flower, to kick a ball*) …
>
> Close your eyes again and remember … what do you hear … and see … and what do you feel … when you are learning well like that?
>
> … and notice what it's like …
>
> … when you are learning at your best …
>
> … and when you are learning at your best like that … it's … like … what?

I watch to see all the children are engaged and ready for the next part of the input before I move on. If it seems appropriate, I will give more time for them to notice what is felt, heard or seen. I may ask children to notice 'whereabouts' they are feeling, hearing or seeing (i.e. is it on the outside or the inside of their body?).

# Creating optimal conditions

It's important to create conditions in the room which allow the children to relax, let go and fully engage with imagining. Exactly how you do this will vary from time to time and from class to class, and no doubt you will have developed your own ways to do this with a class. The key strategy for setting the tone – and the best tip I can give you – is to relax, let go and engage with the process yourself, and cue the other adults in the room to do the same. This is not a time for a teaching assistant to get on with administrative tasks because it will distract children and destroy the focus.

During the input, my teaching assistant moves quietly around the class, inconspicuously 'cueing in' children who need extra support by whispering instructions, signing or showing them through gesture. If necessary, I move among the children as I deliver the input, supporting individuals. But this is not usually necessary if the children are well-prepared. The whole thing takes around four minutes.

# Drawing their imagining

When the children open their eyes I ask them to draw what they have imagined. They work away quietly at their drawings. This is a silent time because I want each child to record their own imagining: to draw *just* what they have imagined and nothing more. And because I want them to attend to the details in their own imagination, I don't want them to share ideas with other children at this stage. The time for sharing will come later. I allow 10 to 15 minutes for them to complete their drawings.

# Expressing it in words

Younger children (Years 1 and 2) share their drawings on a one-to-one basis with my teaching assistant or me at convenient moments during the day. As each child talks about their drawing, we ask clean questions and we scribe a description of their learning at my best metaphor, in their own words. It can take a couple of minutes for each child to explain their ideas, therefore it can take up to an hour of adult time.

Here are a few examples:

> When I'm learning at my best I'm like a fireman, climbing up a ladder to grab all the stuff I need to learn.

When I'm learning at my best I'm like a coloured butterfly. With my wings I sweep everything I don't know into my body and then I know it.

When I'm learning at my best I'm like when it's Christmas and I'm wishing and I'm opening all the presents.

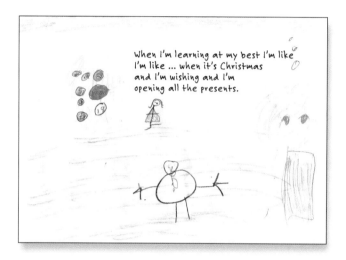

## Supporting each other

Older children (Year 3 and above) produce a drawing in the same way as the younger children. They go on to work with a talk-partner using DDQs to develop their drawings further, adding additional details to their drawings as they go. Sometimes brand new and surprising information emerges. If older children become deeply engaged with questioning and developing their drawings, I'll let them have all the time they need – usually up to about 30 minutes. Most children are used to working like this by this stage, but if necessary I enlist the help of an experienced child or teaching assistant to demonstrate how to work.

## Time for ideas to percolate

When the children have finished the activity they keep their drawing safely in their drawer (or bag), where they can access it freely to look at it and/or think about it and, if they wish, add to it in the period between this and the next activity. I leave a period of between a day and a week before carrying out the next activity to allow time for the children to assimilate, reflect on and develop their ideas.

# What needs to happen for *me* to be learning at my best?

When everyone has a drawing of what they are like when they are learning at their best and they have had time to explore it, reflect on it and ask and answer clean questions about it, I ask the children, 'What needs to happen for you to be learning at your best like that?'[2]

There are several ways to facilitate this process:

- I work with some children on a one-to-one basis.

- My teaching assistant works with some children on a one-to-one basis.

- Experienced children work in pairs taking it in turns to facilitate their partner: one focuses on their own metaphor drawing, and the other asks them questions to identify necessary conditions.

- Some children prefer to share their drawings with the class:

  > They hold their drawing up and read their description.

  > I/another child read(s) their description for them.

  > I/another child ask(s) questions to ascertain necessary conditions.

  > I/another child write(s) the responses on the board.

- Other children prefer to use a simple worksheet to guide them (like the one on page 82).

---

2   I sometimes add '... in here?' or 'here?' to the end of the question, depending on the needs of the group. This is to ensure their focus is on learning in the classroom rather than in wider contexts – because, of course, their needs may be quite different in non-classroom contexts.

---

What needs to happen for you to be able to be learning at your best in here?

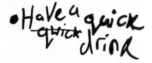

• Have a quick drink

What does it need to be like here, for you to be learning at your best?

• Calmness
• Quiatness
• Slowness

---

You will soon devise a system that suits you and works well in your own context.

When you do this exercise with your class, you and your pupils will learn more about what is needed and valued in your learning environment. Be ready for a few surprises. The following examples offer a taste of the kind of outcomes that emerge.

For me to be learning at my best, I need ...

... to have my friends around.

... it to be cool in here.

... the room to be a bit warmer.

... caring.

... quiet.

... people to whisper.

# A class list of needs (necessary conditions)

When everyone has considered their needs in this way, we work together as a class to make a whole-class list of needs (see below). This takes between 5 and 10 minutes. I've noticed that some themes recur year on year and from class to class, but there are also some big differences – you will notice that Class 3 have far more necessary conditions than the other two classes.

**Class 1**

Darkness, light, cold, warm parts, sun, the edge, space.

**Class 2**

Peaceful, calm, noisy, cheering, quiet, moving, still, big, tiny, flowing colourful, shiny, circle, rhythm, yellow, close, space.

**Class 3**

Very fun, kill the baddies, breeze, fresh air, peaceful, stillness, cheerfulness, get some help, slow moving, still, dynamic balance, colour and sound, flow, relaxed organic structure, quiet, challenging, close race, space (in that room to move around kind of way), getting angry, moonlight, friendly, closeness, calmful, big space to think, really calm, relaxed, bright space, happiness, watching the sun go down, a stretch, sunshine outside, little space, clear air, have a castle, comfortable, to read what I like, to be learning in my own way, very fun.

# What needs to happen in here for *us* to be learning at our best?

Once a whole-class list of necessary conditions has been compiled, children scan for similarities and differences, sorting the list into coherent groupings. There's usually a wide range of needs and many are conflicting. At first it can seem impossible to meet so many incompatible conditions. I ask (often with incredulous curiosity) how all these needs can be met – 'What needs to happen for all this to happen (gesturing to the list) ... for all of us to be learning at our best like this?' – and the children consider, debate and negotiate how to meet the range of conditions.

## Beginning to generate a shared whole-class metaphor

Then I ask, 'What does it need to be like in here? When learning at our best in here ... it's like what?' The children work alone, with a talk-partner or in small groups, to generate ideas about the kind of place the classroom needs to be to support all their learning at my best metaphors and identified needs. Then they pool their ideas. Classes experienced in this approach often share ideas in an open forum without working in pairs or small groups first.

---

### Practice tip

There are lots of methods for groups to share ideas and I expect you will have your own preferences, or you might want to explore some new ones. Whichever method you choose, ensure you are not leading them in their thinking but offer your ideas as a member of the learning team – and include your teaching assistants as team members too. If (and when) children begin to take up the running with the questioning, embrace it – because it heralds the emergence of a self-organising learning team.

---

I offer the problem up to the class and follow their lead, facilitating with clean questions, as they work together to develop a classroom metaphor that will accommodate everyone. This can take up to 30 minutes or sometimes more if the debate and negotiations are substantial.

Here are some snippets of negotiation taken from the three classes featured above.

## Class 1

Tom: When I am learning at my best I feel like a spaceship and my world is surrounded by darkness.

Me: Where would you place your world?

Tom: (*Gestures to a place in the classroom*)

Linda: I want to put my star on the earth.

Tom: That's OK as long as it's not too near and won't interfere with the darkness.

In this instance, when it came to how warm or cool it should be, the class took a vote. There followed a jolly good discussion about whereabouts the metaphors should be placed on a display in the classroom. One child had a raging bull and another had a dragonfly. One child advised the other on her choice of placement, 'If you put it there, that bull might tread on it!'

## Class 2

Loud and still. Close and space. The children began to discuss 'how we can have all of that together in one room'. I brought their attention to their metaphor drawings and as we all looked at them, I wondered aloud:

What does grasshopper need to be able to jump? What does butterfly need to sweep like that?

How can we have this, when grasshopper needs to jump and butterfly needs to sweep? How can we have all of it?

What does it need to be like in here (*gesturing around the classroom*)?

Some children began to describe their ideas and soon everyone was sharing.

It needs to be indoors because people want to dance.

How can it be inside when somebody wants to swim?

They could dance outdoors. They could dance on the beach.

Sid could do her digging in the sand.

The grasshopper needs grass.

We need a mountain for the fireman to climb.

What about the bowler?

I will stand at the top of the mountain and bowl my ball right down the middle. I want to get a strike!

The butterfly needs sky to fly.

## Class 3

| | |
|---|---|
| Charlie: | Where are the bluebirds going to be? |
| Fern: | They're going to be just in the middle. |
| Me: | And when bluebirds ... how many bluebirds? |
| Fern: | Three or two. |
| Me: | Three or two ... and what determines whether three or two? |
| Fern: | I think two because then it will leave enough room for everything else. |
| Me: | OK, two ... then it will leave enough room for everything else ... and two bluebirds just in the middle. Here? |
| Fern: | Yes. |
| Eva: | ... and one butterfly. |
| Me: | Oh ... and one butterfly ... and what kind of butterfly? |
| Eva: | A stripy and spotty one. |
| Me: | And whereabouts? |
| Eva: | I want it kinda up there ... lower than the spaceship. |
| Me: | ... and up there ... lower than the spaceship ... and is that OK for everybody else? |
| Chorus: | Yes! Yes! No! |

| | |
|---|---|
| Paul: | No, because I need my fireball in about that area. |
| Me: | Paul says he needs his fireball in about that area. |
| Paul: | ... because it needs to be able to crash into the spikes. |
| Me: | And when Paul needs his fireball in about that area because it needs to be able to crash into the spikes, and Eva wants it kinda up there, lower than the spaceship ... what needs to happen? |
| Eva: | Mine can be a little bit higher ... but still underneath the spaceship. |
| Paul: | Oh yeah ... thanks. |
| Me: | And is there anything else? (*they interrupt*) |
| Eva: | No. |
| Paul: | No, that's good. |

# Working metaphorically and considering each other's needs

Often children begin by making suggestions that meet only their own needs, but in time they begin to take the needs of others into account – there's a natural emergence of cooperative working. You can see this happening in some of the examples above (e.g. the bull and the dragonfly). They are familiar with each other's metaphors and they have shared necessary conditions, so they have plenty of information to support their thinking. It's lovely to see how considerate they can be as they take account of each other's needs through engagement with their metaphors.

Interestingly, the children are more easily able to assert their needs or those of others when they work symbolically like this. Timid children are more able to speak out about the needs of their butterfly or their shining star than to ask for themselves, and children who might otherwise use aggressive behaviour to get their needs met are more able to negotiate with respect. The children are more readily able to appreciate and reason from the perspective of others when they are working metaphorically. This is an important benefit of working in metaphor.

## Learning at our best in here ... *it's* like what?

As the children negotiate their needs being met through metaphor, they take into account all kinds of attributes – near and far, light and dark, loud and quiet, hard and soft, light and heavy, moving and still, angles, curves, colour, size, shape and more – and sooner or later a class metaphor begins to emerge. The children often become engrossed, negotiating small details and making sure it's a good fit for everyone's needs. I support them if necessary by keeping track of their ideas or recording notes on the board, but often by this stage one or more of the children has taken on this role as the class begins to buzz as a community of learners.

As they reflect on all they have been considering I ask, '... and when all of that ... *this here* (gesturing to their metaphor drawings on display and the lists of necessary conditions) ... is like what?' And as children take it in turns to share their ideas, a class metaphor is created.

## A class metaphor emerges

Beginning with a rough-and-ready sketch on the board, the children (or I) jot down ideas as they arise, and none of us can predict what will emerge. The children use marker pens to indicate whereabouts on the class metaphor they would like their symbol (their learning at my best metaphor) to be, and changes are negotiated until everyone's symbol has a place on the whole-class shared metaphor drawing.

## Practice tip

This is the part of the process when it's crucially important to remember you have to trust the process. At times it can seem as though it's going round in circles, it gets stuck or you will feel it's going nowhere. It can be overwhelmingly tempting to help the children by making suggestions or giving hints. Don't rescue them. Don't hurry in the interest of pace. This is all part of the creative process. *Trust* the process. *Stay clean*. So often the most creative ideas follow what seem to be the worst impasses.

# Class 1's metaphor

One child wanted darkness all around but another child's learning at my best metaphor was stars. This was problematic because when stars are present, their light impinges on darkness. The two children put their minds together and came up with a solution. They decided to place the stars far over to the right-hand side of the display where they could shine without obliterating the darkness. Their positioning was precise to within one centimetre: '*There* … not there.'

Class 1's metaphor evolved into an earth with three regions – polar icecaps, the edge and warmer parts in the middle. Stars were carefully placed so they wouldn't melt the ice caps or encroach on the darkness, which was entirely to one side of the earth – the far side from the sun, obviously!

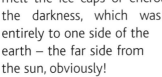

# Class 2's metaphor

You can see in the picture below how the bowler has a place right on the summit of the mountain with the skittles halfway down. The class agreed that it was OK for the symbol to be placed there. The fireman climbs his ladder on one side of the mountain, while the butterfly is placed high in the sky, above the sun 'shining on' (the child's words).

# Class 3's metaphor

This transcript shows how the metaphor landscape evolved.

Me:     So that's the challenge! How can we have all of this ... big space, small space, closeness, room to move, watching the sun go down ...?

Jake:   Impossible!

Me:     Yeah ... it can seem impossible and that's our challenge ... because this is what we need ... if we take our whole class together ... these are the things that people need ... and so how can we have all of this in here (*gesturing around the room*)? That's what we're going to be thinking about now.

So when we do have all of this ... very fun, kill the baddies, breeze, fresh air, peaceful, stillness, cheerfulness, get some help, slow moving, still, dynamic balance, colour and sound, flow, relaxed organic structure, quiet, challenging, close race, space (in that room to move around kind of way), getting angry, moonlight, friendly, closeness, calmful, big space to think, really calm, relaxed, bright space, happiness, watching the sun go down, a stretch, sunshine outside, little space, clear air, have a castle, comfortable, to read what I like, to be learning in my own way, very fun ... all of this ... in here ... it's like what?

Close your eyes just for a moment ... and imagine just what it's like in here when it's all of this ... notice what you are imagining. Notice what you see ... what you hear ... what you feel ... what you smell ... and taste. And now take one minute to tell your talk-partner what you have imagined.

Would anyone like to share?

Jill:   Well, I don't know if it would work but I was thinking, though, how we could have *closeness* and *room to move* at the same time.

Me:     How we could have closeness and room to move at the same time ... yes, come on then ... how could we?

Jill:     I don't know if it would work but we could like have two cardboard shields over there and a weak space so people who want space to move can like push through the weak space and people who want closeness could stay in-between the barriers.

Me:     Can you show me, here and here what you mean (*referring to two areas Jill had been pointing to*). Two shields did you say?

Jill:     Yes, two cardboard strips like over here and like here, and some weak spaces ... like we can just cut it out and like keep it there.

Me:     I don't know what that would look like yet. Can you see where Jill's pointing and moving? ... She's thinking of somewhere here. (*Jill moves around the room pointing out the special arrangement of her barriers and weak spaces*)

    OK ... anyone else with ideas? (*I field lots of ideas from the class*) Wow! We've got a whole list: Lollypop Land, a machine that makes metal robots and fires guns, LEGOLAND with dungeons, Sweetie Land, grassy plains, Apple Tree Farm, somewhere where we can shoot arrows through the window, park and big garden with lots of flowers, pool and ocean.

    Think of yourself when *you are* learning at your best, what do you need?

Jenny:     A garden with lots of flowers would be fine for me because I am a butterfly.

Me:     Put up your hand if that would be fine for you.

    Put up your hand if it would not be fine for you.

    ... and what needs to happen for it to be fine for you?

John:     A spaceship hovering above the garden trying to capture me.

Me:     Anyone else?

Jake:     I need a place where there are loads of spikes.

Me:     ... and what kind of spikes?

Jake:     Sharp ones ... just outside the castle.

Me:     ... and is there anything else?

Jerry:     I need apple trees.

Me:     So we have all that … the castle, the barriers and weak spaces
        and apple trees … and grassy plain and sharp spikes and a garden
        with flowers and a spaceship hovering above it and all of that.
        We're going to have that in here (*gesturing around the room*)
        and I don't know where … so whereabouts?

During the afternoon we rearranged the classroom together to form castle walls, with windows that looked out over the ocean (a wall display) and a small doorway with a portcullis for children to squeeze through into a small courtyard space which they had visualised earlier. A large part of the classroom became the inside of the castle and visible through another window (a wall display – see below) were the grassy plains, a flower garden, apple trees and so on, so everything was included.

I find that older children (i.e. Years 5 and 6) love collaborating to design effective, functional learning environments like this as much as younger children do. They quickly become invested in the development and maintenance of their surroundings when they have designed them themselves – they then take the initiative in promoting their own learning culture.

## Making the whole-class metaphor collage

Once the metaphor landscapes have been developed and we have arrived at an overarching class metaphor that is agreeable to all class members (children and adults), the children work in teams to make a collage of it, sourcing materials from available class resources or from home. There are usually several areas in the classroom where the collage can be displayed and the children choose the best place by identifying alternatives and then taking a vote (thus experiencing first hand how the democratic process works at the same time).

## Children make and place their symbols

The children make 3D models of their learning at my best symbols and bring them to be placed on the collage. As they prepare to place their symbol, I use a clean approach (based on a process known as a Clean Start devised by David Grove) to facilitate them saying, 'Place that where it needs to be.' And as they place their symbol, I ask:

 … and is that in the right space?

 … and is that at the right height?

 … and is that at the right angle?

 … and is that (facing) in the right direction?

Children make adjustments to the position of their symbol in response to each question (sometimes fine adjustments). After each change I ask the series of questions again so they can check if their symbol is now in the right place. We continue with this pattern of adjusting position, asking questions, readjusting position, asking questions, readjusting position, asking questions ... until the position of the symbol is just right and the child is completely satisfied with it.

Occasionally a child realises that his or her symbol needs to be placed in another part of the classroom (or, in the case of one symbol, a spaceship, floating in space – this was achieved with fine strings attached to the ceiling). Having their exact requirements honoured like this can be a new experience for some children. More often than not they are expected to forgo, compromise or relinquish what they want. When they know they will be listened to and their choices respected, children become increasingly discriminating in those choices.

## And what difference does all this make?

Although the whole process is conducted through the medium of metaphor, often tangible changes in behaviour follow these whole-class shared metaphor exercises which are astonishing and delightful.

In the case of the dragonfly and the bull, the child whose symbol was the bull had a habit of encroaching on other children's space and the child whose symbol was the dragonfly would often be at the mercy of him and was powerless to change this pattern of behaviour. Following the creation of the class metaphor landscape, with all the negotiating it entailed, the first child became more sensitive to other people's personal space and the second became more assertive – selecting comfortable places to sit rather than feeling cramped and suffering in silence. Real-life behaviour was not discussed, but through the medium of metaphor, attitudes shifted and behaviour changed.

Every time I do this activity the whole-class metaphors that emerge are different. The journey taken to arrive at the metaphor is different and the quality of the atmosphere in the room is different (sometimes still and thoughtful, sometimes energised and invigorated), but the negotiation process is much the same

– respectful – and as a result something changes. So it's the journey itself, the process the class goes through (which has a clean philosophy embedded in every step), which appears to make the difference rather than the pathway taken or the specific metaphors which emerge en route.

# How long does it take?

You may be thinking that this is taking up a lot of classroom time, and you'd be right, but the benefits of this far outweigh the time taken – as you'll see. It may also seem that this approach could take valuable time and attention away from the curriculum, but in fact it aligns well with personal, social and health education (PSHE) objectives and can be integrated into the art curriculum.

It can be completed in the time you would ordinarily allow for settling a new class into routines and expectations, so it will take up less time than you might imagine. And, having established an independent learning culture in your class early on, you will spend far less time during the year dealing with disruptions which makes it a sound investment. The table below gives an approximate time breakdown of all the activities.

| Developing a whole-class metaphor | | |
|---|---|---|
| **Focus** | **Activity** | **Approximate time taken** |
| Prior experience of the learning at my best activity for teaching assistant(s)<br><br>To support them for their role in the demonstration session | Imagining | 30 minutes |
| When I'm learning at my best I'm like what?<br>Metaphor | Imagining<br>Drawing | 4 minutes<br>10–15 minutes |

| Developing a whole-class metaphor | | |
|---|---|---|
| Focus | Activity | Approximate time taken |
| Model developing a learning at my best metaphor using a teaching assistant or experienced child as a demo subject – if necessary | Imagining<br>Using clean questions | 4 minutes |
| Develop learning at my best metaphor drawing | Using clean questions<br>Describing (verbal or written description) | 1–2 minutes each (one-to-one with an adult) or 15–30 minutes (talk-partners) |
| Make personal learning metaphor | Making 3D symbol | 15–30 minutes (this can be done as an art activity in which case you may take longer) |
| What needs to happen for *me* to be learning at my best like that (in here)?<br>Identify necessary conditions (needs) | Using clean questions (working one-to-one with an adult scribe, with a talk-partner or independently using a worksheet)<br>Communicating needs to class | 10 minutes |
| Share needs (necessary conditions) with class | Making class list of needs | 5–10 minutes |

| Developing a whole-class metaphor | | |
|---|---|---|
| **Focus** | **Activity** | **Approximate time taken** |
| What needs to happen for *us* to be learning at our best (in here)?<br>Necessary conditions | Sorting and categorising necessary conditions | 10 minutes |
| What needs to happen in here for *us* to be learning at our best?<br>Consider needs with regards to others' needs and our class environment | Negotiating with regard to the needs of each person's personal learning metaphor | 30 minutes – or as long as it takes<br>These two activities often merge into one as the negotiating often inspires ideas for the overarching metaphor. Sometimes we leave a day or two between the two activities to allow ideas to percolate – it depends on the group |
| And when learning at our best in here ... it's like what?<br>Shared class metaphor | Brainstorming to create a class metaphor which meets everyone's needs<br>Recording ideas on the board as they emerge (adult or child) | |
| Make whole-class metaphor | Making class metaphor collage | 30 minutes – or as long as you choose. Small groups can work on it in succession so everyone is involved |
| Place symbol where it needs to be | Placing 3D symbol on class metaphor collage | ½–1 minute each (one-to-one during odd moments) |

Once the whole-class metaphor is in place as a wall display, you can refer to it verbally or through gesture (e.g. a glance, a point of the finger, a sweep of the hand) throughout the term or year to:

- Remind your class of the whole-class vision.

- Motivate individuals.

- Remind the class (or individuals) of the varying needs within the class.

- Manage behaviour – reminding children of expectations.

When teaching, I set conditions for the week, for the day or for a particular task by gesturing and saying, '... and what needs to happen for this?' If ever the working atmosphere deteriorates, I might say:

> ... and this (*gesturing around the room, at what's happening*)
>
> ... and this (*gesturing to the whole-class metaphor drawing*)
>
> ... and what needs to happen for this? (*gesturing again to the drawing*)

Or I might ask:

> ... and what's happening right now? (*looking around the room at what's happening – or not happening*)
>
> ... and what needs to happen for us to be learning at our best? (*gazing towards the collage*)

Sometimes I'll invite them to get smoothly and swiftly back on track by using fewer words and gesturing instead:

> And this! (*gesturing with a sweep of the arm to indicate everything that's happening in the room*)
>
> And this! (*gesturing to the learning at our best class metaphor*)

And then I shrug, with a questioning 'What needs to happen?' expression on my face. The children invariably know exactly what needs to happen and they make the adjustments accordingly – a picture saves a thousand words.

The first few methods above invite verbal responses and usually a discussion or debate ensues. The final method re-establishes a good learning culture quickly and without any need for discussion, so it doesn't break the flow of the learning activity.

# Learning principles

When you have a whole-class metaphor drawing, developed as a shared understanding and which takes everyone's learning needs into account like this, you have a symbol that embraces all your class rules. It's a symbol that carries a breadth and depth of meaning and intimacy which exceeds anything that a list of rules can accomplish because it describes so much more than can be easily put into words. It stands as a visual reminder of everything we know about each other in class: what we're like, what we need and what we would like to have happen.

It demonstrates a shared ownership of the learning environment – symbolising the learning principles by which we all operate. It can foster a deep level of respect for diversity within the class and beyond as class members (adults and children) begin to work according to these principles to support their own and others' learning.

# What happens in terms 2 and 3?

At the beginning of the spring and summer terms we sometimes do a new learning at my best collage, but not always. It can help to re-establish the learning environment in a class that needs to refocus after the holidays. Occasionally metaphors change or children discover more detail about them, but usually they remain the same.

There is little need for protracted introductions in the second and third terms as the children are already familiar with the process. I facilitate a whole class with a brief introduction to get them started before inviting them to complete the task independently. Usually they can facilitate each other by this stage and will only need minimal support as they are proficient in asking the questions.

The following is a transcript of a brief introduction. It shows how swift the process of accessing learning at my best states can be, if the class is familiar with it and the questions are asked of the whole class at once.

# A swift whole-class introduction

OK … so you've had a good morning. Who's done some good learning this morning? (*most hands are raised – my teaching assistant knows to target support on those who don't raise their hands*) You have worked hard, done some lovely work and you have learned something new … learning well … and you have given yourselves a pat on the back!

… and I want you to take a moment now to think about times when you have been learning at your best. And you are thinking about *all* the times you have learned brilliantly like that … and you can close your eyes … as soon as you wish … and remember a time … when you were learning at your best.

… and noticing what that's like … what you see … what you hear … what you feel … and I don't want you to draw that yet, until you have noticed all you need to notice about you, learning at your best … now … draw.

The children then draw themselves learning at their best. When the drawings are complete, they have them on their desks to refer to while I ask the following questions. My teaching assistant writes the questions on a flip chart so the children can keep track of them, and we can refer back to them during the summary at the end.

When you are learning at your best like that …

What's that like? … tell your talk-partner … quickly now.

… and is there anything else about that? (*get a sense of it*) … tell your partner.

… and whereabouts is that? … tell your partner.

… and where? … tell your partner.

... and that (*gesturing to indicate the attribute they're thinking about*) there ... does that have a shape or a size? ... tell your partner.

... or a colour? ... tell your partner.

... and ... colour ... size ... shape ... and there ... (*repeating the earlier gesture*) and learning at your best ... (*pointing to the recordings of the questions on the flip chart*)

... and is there anything else ... when you are learning at your best like that?

Tell your talk-partner.

OK, now get that down ... on paper ... draw it or write it ... or whatever you need to do to ... get that down now.

---

## Practice tip

- **Tone:** Imagine the children are accessing a 'great place' (or a 'great state'). Be curious about their metaphor landscape and let this show in your tone of voice – let it be encouraging and curious.

- **Pause:** Allow time for the children to engage their imaginations.

- **Accept:** Accept whatever comes up for them without judgement. There's no right or wrong, or better or worse.

- **Observe:** Use your sensory acuity to notice when children have accessed new information and alter the timing of your delivery to match the pace of their imagining.

---

## Sharing the learning: learning at our best in assembly

In our school, each class takes a turn to present an assembly to share their learning with the rest of the school. Every child is involved, most teachers and teaching assistants attend and parents are invited too. One of my classes planned to talk about learning at my best metaphors during their assembly – how the metaphors reveal individual differences and how we accommodate and embrace differences in the classroom. They anticipated it would be difficult for the audience to appreciate the effectiveness of the metaphor work through description alone, so they asked me to lead a brief learning at my best session with the whole school and the visiting parents. They wanted the audience to experience what they were sharing. A snippet of their assembly plan appears in the box below, followed by an example from another class who asked Isabel to describe how they embrace the diversity in the group.

---

Samuel: This term we're thinking even more about how we learn well. We drew pictures of ourselves learning at our best and then we described it in words.

(*Everyone holds up metaphors and reads them out*)

Samuel: Notice how different we all are.

Me: Perhaps you would like to have a go? Remember a time when you were learning something new really well. I don't know if you can remember just how you felt, and what you could hear and see then when you learned quickly and easily … now … notice what it's like when you are learning easily, when you are learning at your best … now … take a moment to notice … when you are learning at your best … that's … like … what?

Give the audience time for experiencing, then invite them to share their experiences with each other – ask a few clean questions of some of the children and adults. Invite them to notice how different we all are: 'You might like to share your differences with each other when you get back to your classrooms.'

Samuel: Because we are all so different, we thought about how we can all be comfortable in our classroom together and learn at our best in our different ways.

Kathryn: We thought about … when we are all learning at our best, this is like what? And we thought what it would be like in our classroom.

---

(*Show chart: peaceful, calm, noisy, cheering, quiet, moving, still, big, tiny, flowing colourful, shiny, circle, rhythm, yellow … music, dancing, singing, sun, stream … river … flowing to the sea, whirlpool, purple haze*)

Emma:   We made models of ourselves learning at our best and put them on the picture.

(*Hold up models*)

Isabel:   At the start of each term we remember how we learn at our best. Everyone is different. Some people need peace and quiet; some people need space to move; some people need to make a noise and talk about their work; some people need fresh air and some people need a cosy, warm space. We try to make sure that everyone has what they need – even if we don't quite understand it.

Preparing and then sharing what they have come to know and understand helps to reinforce the learning for the children as they introduce it to others. When the class work together on projects like this, they are challenged to think from a metacognitive perspective as they reflect on learning and take account of (and plan for) the learning needs of others.

## Reflecting on learning: a research group emerges

As awareness of their learning processes rises children become more engaged. Seven-year-old Tom, for instance, reflected on the question, 'And is there anything else about (…)?' and concluded that it functions both as an open and a closed question. He was very keen to investigate the questions further.

Tom was one of a group of children from across the year group who had been meeting once a week for a learning challenge. He decided to share this with the group at breaktime. They were all keen to monitor the effectiveness of the questions in different curriculum areas and feed back their thoughts about them.

Tom arranged for the group to meet up and discuss the idea. A mini research and development group was born.

Up until then I had been leading the weekly challenge sessions using clean facilitation. Feedback from an external moderator who observed the group in action encouraged us to forge ahead: 'The formation of a group which promotes gifted and talented opportunities is a wonderful feature of the school's engagement with children's needs and interests.' Now the children were reflecting on the questions themselves, aiming to discover where the questions are most effective and where they are less effective. They were beginning to provide feedback on the questions I had been using to facilitate them. I asked the children:

> And, if you are happy to, I'd like you to tell me whether the questions are helpful or not, whether the questions make you think or not, when/where they are helpful or not helpful.

We all agreed that reflecting and feeding back thoughts about the questioning would be an optional extra in these weekly sessions (it was a free choice) and if anyone didn't want to take up this option it wouldn't affect their work on the central learning challenge. They were all keen to participate. Then I posed their learning challenge question:

> This project is a chance to challenge yourself – a chance for you to choose. If there was something that you have always wanted to do or find out about ... this is your chance. And so with this project now ... what would you like to have happen?

Here are their responses:

> Find out how many seconds in a year.
>
> Find out how many people ... like ... certain categories ... (interviews).
>
> You know how I quite like God, I want to find out how many gods there are.
>
> ... and when ... what kind of how many is that?
>
> Yeah, and where they come from.
>
> Make a film about what's going on in school, about children's learning ... asking individual children things ... no subject, although about children's learning ... I don't want to ask about the school bazaar or plays, but about the children and how they learn in school.

Drawing and finding out. I don't mind what about – any subject.

I then introduced them to the idea of thought mapping. I showed them how to put 'our project' in the middle and then add thoughts to the branches as they go.

By then it was almost time to stop but they were eager to carry on. They had decided they wanted to work together to make a film about gods and they wanted to calculate how many seconds it has been since the time people believed in specific gods (e.g. Roman gods). I couldn't imagine what this project would develop into, but I did know that I would need to move fast in order to organise some thought-mapping software and film-making equipment.

Before they left I asked, 'When I asked you, "What would you like to have happen?" … what was that like for you?' Here are their responses …

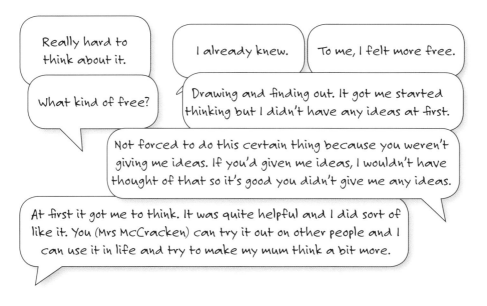

This chapter has given an insight and a practical overview of how clean questions, combined with an understanding of metaphor, can be introduced and used throughout the year to develop a cooperative and respectful learning culture in class. Once you begin to use the questions in your own class, you will develop ways that suit you, your children and the context you are working in.

# Chapter 5

# Mental Models and Misconceptions

We must place ourselves inside the heads of our students and try to understand as far as possible the sources and strengths of their conceptions.

**Howard Gardner, *The Unschooled Mind* (1991)**

When we think about our pupils' understanding, their behaviour or their reasoning, it's commonplace to think in terms of 'what' and 'why':

- *What* do you know, and *why* do you know it?

- *What* do you think, and *why* do you think it?

- *What* did you do, and *why* did you do it?

This chapter explores how to model children's ways of making sense of the world by finding out 'what' and 'how'. Clean questions are eminently suited to the task.

- *What* do you know, and *how* do you know it?

- *What* do you think, and *how* do you think it?

- *What* do you do, and *how* do you do it?

This process considers what actually goes on in children's heads and how we (and they) can better catch a glimpse of it. As you read on, continue to reflect on metaphors and their impact on learning as you consider the practice of modelling.

---

Modelling is a fundamental part of teaching and learning but the terms 'model' and 'modelling' are used in various ways. The verb 'to model' is used as a synonym of the verb 'to demonstrate'. According to the *Chambers Dictionary* (2008) modelling is 'to form after a model; to shape; to make a model or copy of; the act or art of making a model of something'. The *Penguin English Dictionary* (2003) gives at least 14 different uses for the term.

As teachers:

- We use modelling in computing, science, maths and design and technology to convey information about the world in succinct form – models show how things work.

- We model aspects of reading and writing in literacy so our pupils can imitate and thereby learn a skill – models demonstrate.

- We model the kind of behaviour we want pupils to adopt – models exemplify.

- We operate according to models of good practice in our teaching roles – models evolve.

In bottom-up modelling, the details are *described* – for example, disassembly (reverse engineering) is used to reveal underlying components, structures and processes in maths, science and design and technology. The details are not known until the modelling process reveals them.

In top-down modelling approaches, the details are *prescribed* – for example, in biological classification systems where the subject (e.g. dolphin) fits into a predetermined category (i.e. mammal).

If you are a teacher, you will have a professional familiarity with most, if not all, of these notions of models and modelling.

Day to day, teachers place a lot of their attention on trying to figure out what is going on in children's minds. What do they know already? Do they get it or don't they? Where has he gone wrong? How has she gone wrong? What do I need to do next in order for them to understand?

In order to answer these questions, teachers construct hypothetical models of children's thinking: they make mental models of the children's mental models. Mental modelling is important to reasoning and to the reflective and critical thinking skills used by children as they engage in the curriculum. It's the same process used by teachers as they model children's thinking applied for a different purpose.

Here is how the process is described by Maria Salett Biembengut (2007: 451) in a study for the 14th International Commission on Mathematical Instruction on modelling and applications in mathematics education:

> In their everyday life children perceive their environment, obtain information and select from it, compare it to what they already know, and after assimilation, confer significance to the various scenarios that surround them. The child is always interactively researching everything within his grasp. His imagination surpasses the limits of the image, leading him to create symbols or objects and to form ideas, giving form, colour and sense to the world in which he lives.

Biembengut goes on to explain how this mental process passes through three stages – perception, comprehension and signification – where a child's sensations or perceptions produce ideas (imagination) which, when linked to prior comprehension 'may be transformed into *significance*, a mental model that results into understanding'. It is through creating and continuously building on representations (mental models) of the world around them that children learn how to 'be' in the world.

Although mental models are not reality, their structure has to match reality to some degree if they are to be useful. Obviously, you don't keep your local town (the real one) in your head; you create a representation of it. The structure of this representation will match the real-world town but it won't actually *be* the real-world town. If the match is a good one then you will be able to use it to navigate. If it's not good then its usefulness will be limited. If there's no match then it won't be of any use at all.

You are probably aware from your own use of models that a single model never matches the reality in its entirety or in all contexts. For example, a map may be useful in some situations because of its clear simplicity, while a satellite view of the same terrain (with its life-like pictorial information) may be useful in others. A satellite view is not the best choice if you want to navigate a route by car – it contains too much information.

Misconceptions can arise when children's models are not well-matched to real-life counterparts or where there is a contextual match (or a partial match) and the child generalises beyond the scope of their model. Some examples of these misconceptions are listed in the table below.

## Misconceptions related to plants and plant systems

Grades 6–8: ages 11–14 (Angus, 1981)

- Children who were able to correctly classify an item as an animal were also able to classify the animal as having bones or not having bones. The major exceptions were the tortoise, frog and shark.

- A significant number of children regard heavenly phenomena as living, such as the sun, clouds, rain and wind. All of these phenomena move and are associated with life.

- Another group of items commonly listed by children as living are those associated with people and their actions, such as planes, bells, cars, clocks and fire.

## Misconceptions related to rain

Grades 1–5: ages 6–11 (Za'rour, 1976)

- Many students did not think rain came from the sea.

- Half of the students in the sample believed that rain is in the clouds before it rains.

## Misconceptions related to the nature of light

Grade 1–12: ages 6–18 (Stephens, 1994)

- A colour filter adds colour to a white beam.

- The eye is the active agent in gathering light rather than being just a receiver of reflected light.

- Shadows are independent of the object causing them.

- Magnifying glasses make the light 'bigger' (i.e. there is more light on the side of the lens opposite the source).

When misconceptions like this happen it's easy for them to go unnoticed by the pupil and the teacher because (a) if there is a partial match they will work at some level, some of the time and/or in some contexts, (b) they are mental constructs so they are hidden from view and (c) our assumptions mask critical detail.

Misconceptions may be personal or cultural. As a society we deliberately create misconceptions, such as Father Christmas, the Tooth Fairy and the Easter Bunny ... but let's not go there! A personal example of my own is that, as a young child, I believed that all houses were 100 feet high. Although I could see that some houses stood taller than others and the rooftops of bungalows were much lower than those of houses, my belief remained solid.

Every once in a while my dad would gather me and my siblings together, measure us and record our heights by marking them on the living room doorframe. One day, as my dad stood in the doorway gouging our heights into the frame, I began to do some measuring of my own. I knew he was 6 feet tall. I eyed him up and down, compared him to the height of the room and estimated that the room was probably around 8 feet high. I figured that two rooms would be 16 feet high and factoring in the loft as well, the house would probably be about 24 feet high. I went outside and imagined how many dads (stacked on top of each other) it would take to reach the roofline. It was definitely less than five, so the house was definitely less than 30 feet high.

Something seemed wrong. I began to check other houses in the vicinity using similar rudimentary estimations and concluded that houses actually come in a range of heights. I had held my misconception for a couple of years. The mistaken belief changed following a moment of cognitive dissonance which led to a period of investigation – I collected lots of evidence which contradicted the belief.

A cultural example from the past is that for centuries people thought disease was caused by a miasma (a poisonous gas that could be recognised by its foul smell) and could be cured or prevented by masking the smell. Since the latter part of the 19th century, it would have been considered a misconception if you thought miasmas caused diseases because germ theory had begun to replace these earlier ideas.

A more recent example is the change in our understanding of the nature of the brain, largely due to information made available by neuroscientists and brain imaging technology. The idea that brain plasticity continues throughout life is a relatively new concept and supersedes the idea that 'old dogs can't learn new tricks'.

## Practice task

You will probably have examples of your own past misconceptions. You might find it interesting to revisit one or two of them now and identify:

- How you came to realise each misconception was a misconception.

- How much time went by before you realised it was a misconception.

- What triggered your realisation.

- How your updated conception is the same as your misconception.

- How your updated conception is different from your misconception.

Considering how easy it is for mistakes like this to happen – and what can happen when new concepts are built upon erroneous ones – it's easy to see how whole systems of understanding can be built upon mental models that have shaky foundations, which then result in insecure learning.

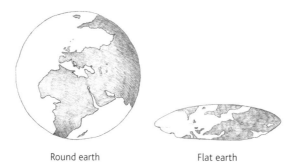

Round earth                    Flat earth

In a classroom context, it's important to be able to check out the mental models children are creating because (a) these models underpin their understanding, (b) they can be more useful or less useful and, significantly, (c) they can be at the root of many misconceptions. Clean Language offers an effective way to check out the subtleties of mental models from the bottom up. You and your pupils can use the questions to focus attention systematically to unveil models, reveal their structure and find out how they work.

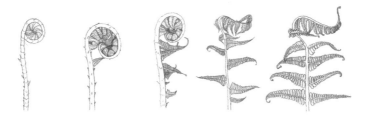

The method can be used in all areas of the curriculum – you can model all kinds of structures, mechanisms, processes, biological systems, ecological systems, information systems and human systems (strategies, skills, performance, etc.). When modelling people's thought processes, attention is directed to particular kinds of sensory, conceptual and symbolic information, as shown in the table below.

| | **Sensory information** | **Conceptual information** | **Symbolic information** |
|---|---|---|---|
| **Type of information** | Sensory information: things you can see or hear | Verbal descriptions | Metaphors, symbols, relationships in space and time |
| **Focus of the modelling** | Modelling what children do, e.g. behaviours, skills, social interaction, working practices | Modelling what children think: thinking processes, beliefs, strategies | Modelling what children's behavioural and thinking processes are like<br><br>The organisation of their metaphorical landscape |

|  | Sensory information | Conceptual information | Symbolic information |
|---|---|---|---|
| **Examples** | Handwriting: sitting up straight, pen held in standard grip with a soft tension, shoulders dropped (relaxed) | Handwriting: I'm good at handwriting because I concentrate and tell myself to let my hand flow smoothly | Handwriting: My hand is like a feather whipped up on a gentle breeze, flipping and flowing lightly along |

# Modelling and metaphor

Teachers frequently make use of metaphor to aid children's understanding because it helps us to understand and experience 'one kind of thing in terms of another' (Lakoff and Johnson, 1980: 5). Electricity, for example, is often likened to the *flow* of water through pipes – to illustrate the relationship between amps and volts – and also to a *push* travelling along a row of dominos (or row of children), illustrating the movement of energy around a circuit.

As we have seen, metaphors support understanding because at some level the information contained in them marries with their counterparts in reality. Taking the two electrical metaphors above, for example, each describes a different property of electricity and neither of them describes all properties of electricity.

Sometimes the key information is carried in the structure of a metaphor, but more often it's in the attributes of symbols, the relationships between symbols and in patterns of relationships. In the case of the water pipe metaphor for electricity, it's the relationship between the size of the pipe, the speed of flow and the pressure of the water that holds the key information.

Citing George Lakoff, Steven Pinker (2008: 253) points out that metaphors (analogies) are 'aids to reason'. They have long been used to scaffold thinking around engineering and scientific problems and challenges. Importantly he asserts:

For an analogy to be scientifically useful ... the correspondences can't apply to a part of one thing that merely resembles the part of another. They have to apply to the relationships between the parts, and even better, to the relationships between the relationships, and to the relationships between the relationships between the relationships.

## So why do metaphors matter?

Metaphors have an important role to play in teaching and learning because:

- We use them to reason and make predictions.

- They enable us to communicate complex experiences in words.

- They give form to the formless – they make the intangible tangible.

- They frame our perspectives and influence our behaviour.

- They have form – we can notice when they change.

- When they change, our perspectives and ways of being in the world change along with them.

- We commonly understand new ideas by taking known ideas into new topic areas via metaphorical extension.

It's natural to be curious about the metaphors your pupils are forming in class, and in my experience fellow pupils find it fascinating and informative too. Use the following guide (based loosely on Tompkins and Lawley's (2002) Symbolic Modelling process) to model learners' metaphors. Remember to apply all that you have already learned about clean questions and work with a respectful intention. I suggest you practise in one-to-one situations before working with individuals in a classroom context.

## Modelling a metaphor

Identify a metaphor and ask clean questions about it.

Find out *what* and *where*. Use developing questions to reveal the symbols – the elements of the metaphor:

- … and what kind of (…)?
- … and is there anything else about (…)?
- … and whereabouts is (…)?
- … and where is (…)?

This will give form to the symbols and reveal their attributes.

Find out *how*. Use relationship questions to reveal how the symbols relate to each other:

- … and when (…), what happens to (…)?
- … and when (…), where is (…)?
- … and when (…), is there anything else about (…)?
- … and is there a relationship between (…) and (…)?
- … and is (…) the same as or different to (…)?

This will give a sense of the structure of a metaphor landscape – where symbols are in relation to each other and how they relate.

Find out *when* (the sequence of events). Use relationship questions to reveal how symbols relate temporally (over time).

- … and (…) then what happens?
- … and (…) what happens next?
- … and (…) what happens just before (…) and just after (…)? (i.e. between two events in a sequence)

This will give a sense of the sequences of events in a metaphor landscape – it reveals processes. For example, '… and rain, what happens just before *rain*?'

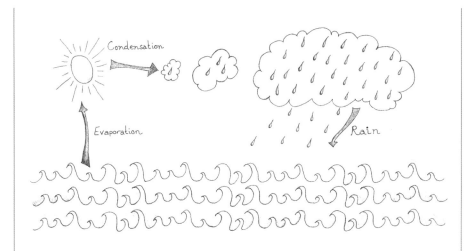

See 'Misconceptions related to rain', page 110.

## Practice task

- Identify a metaphor:

  > You might like to focus on your own electrical metaphor for this exercise.

  > Or you may prefer to choose a metaphor that you are planning to use with your class to support their understanding of an aspect of the curriculum.

  > Or perhaps you would like to develop a resource of your own, such as 'listening at your best'.

- Model the metaphor by following the 'modelling a metaphor' process described on page 116.

The more I model people's processes using Clean Language, the more I'm aware that we are all so delightfully different. Even models that are the same on the surface turn out to be surprisingly different when you look beneath. Take the maths examples below. The problem was 35 − 27 = ? When I used DDQs to drill below the surface, this is what I found:

| | |
|---|---|
| **Child 1** <br> 1. Start on the right. <br> 2. 5 take 7 – you can't do it. <br> 3. Nick 10 off the 3 (which is really 30). <br> 4. Give it to the 5 to make it 15. <br> 5. 7 is 3 away from 10 so add 3 to the 5 ... makes 8. <br> 6. 2 take away 2 equals zero. | |
| **Child 2** <br> 1. I don't bother with borrowing. I count up. <br> 2. 27 add 3 makes it up to 30. <br> 3. Add 5 (to make it up to 35) is 8. | |
| **Child 3** <br> 1. Cross out the 3 and change it to a 2. <br> 2. And then ... I can't remember the rest. <br> 3. We did it. I remember doing it but I can't remember how it goes after that. <br> 4. I know you have to cross the 3 out and change it to a 2. <br> 5. I know you start on the left. | |

Child 4

1. Put 3 on the 27 to make it simple. (But remember it's just temporary. I don't really join it in my head. I just place it on top so it's an even 30.)
2. 35 minus 30 is easy, it's 5.
3. Then I take the 3 and put it up with the 5 which makes 8.

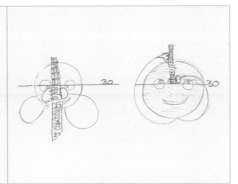

# Making assumptions

Although you know individuals' models are unique, it can still be easy to make assumptions about them without realising it – to slip into a mindset where you think you know what is coming next. Keeping a tight rein on your assumptions as you work (particularly when the subject is familiar to you) is absolutely essential to successful modelling.

I reflected with a colleague on the value of a clean approach, with its potential for clearer communication in relation to assessment procedures like this one.

Sita had answered the question, 'What do you feel like when you or someone else is naughty in class and the teacher is cross?' by picking a smiley face card from a selection of cards with images representing a range of emotions. Despite further instruction in what the images meant (especially the unhappy face) and three more opportunities to pick the 'correct card', she was steadfast in her original choice – the smiley face.

The conclusion (the assessment or the assumption) was that she couldn't correctly match facial expressions with corresponding feelings – until, pointing to the smiley face, she asserted, 'I always laugh when I'm told off – I think it's funny – friends laugh too!' and it became clear she could match them perfectly well. Sita had picked the correct face from the perspective of her own model of classroom life. The mismatch was between the adult's model of how a child might respond in that context and the child's model born of her own experience.

We had seen how easy it can be to arrive at mistaken conclusions in the absence of a little exploration beyond face value. It was a timely reminder of something Einstein once said: 'Most teachers waste their time by asking questions which are intended to discover what a pupil does not know, whereas the true art of questioning has for its purpose to discover what the pupil knows or is capable of knowing' (see Moszkowski, 1921).

(Incidentally, it's common for some children to laugh when they are frightened too; it's a nervous response. So in some contexts the smiley face could denote fear as well.)

Children's experiences are what they are – we can't simply decide what they ought to be. Bottom-up modelling using Clean Language helps to avoid placing children into ready-made categories. It helps reveal what is actually there.

# More about modelling

We have considered conceptual metaphors, metaphors for learning at your best and for listening at your best and you have completed other modelling practices as well. The applications for modelling and Symbolic Modelling are wide ranging. Modelling can be used to:

- Enable pupils to know how they do what they do – and, if required, for them to improve their own processes.

- Elicit processes underlying skills in order to transfer them from one person to another through metaphor.

- Develop group metaphors to enable groups to work together with a common vision.

- Form effective learning communities.

Modelling helps to reveal the structure which underlies children's thinking: it helps you lift the lid and see what is there. You can find examples of the use of modelling and Symbolic Modelling in a range of contexts in Part 2, and if you are interested to learn more about it then have a look at the bibliography.

# Chapter 6
# Facilitating Learning

We must ask, 'What do I (or we) really want?' This sounds simple, but it takes substantial discipline to stop your emotions and anxiety long enough to simply refocus on what matters to you.

Peter Senge, Joseph Jaworski, C. Otto Scharmer
and Betty Sue Flowers, *Presence* (2005)

We have seen in previous chapters how metaphors change and how this can effect changes in real-life perspectives and behaviour – and if you haven't already noticed examples of changes in your own metaphors and considered their effects, I imagine you are becoming aware of these shifts happening now.

For the most part we have talked about changes happening incidentally. Incidental changes occur spontaneously in response to experiences. Modelling (especially Symbolic Modelling) trains attention on particular aspects of experience, and it's out of this awareness that changes arise.

## How does change happen with a clean methodology?

Change can happen in a number of ways:

- As you become more aware of the metaphors you are living by, you naturally begin to reflect on the resulting implications.

- You become more aware that your take on life is just that – your current perspective – and not the unadulterated truth.

- You become more able to switch between perspectives – you become more flexible and you have more choices available to you.

- As you become aware of your own thinking patterns, they exert less of a hold and are more amenable to change.

- You come to appreciate your strengths (and weaknesses) and just how creative you can be.

When you work with a clean approach the children in your class will naturally become more self-aware and reflective in their thinking, and as a consequence of working this way, so will you as you nurture the conditions for learning – for change to happen. As Carl Rogers (2004 [1961]: 15) so astutely observes: 'The curious paradox is that when I accept myself as I am, then I change.'

# Focusing on outcomes

Outcomes are a central part of teaching and learning and I expect you are extremely familiar with objectives, targets and goals (long term, short term, medium term). All of these are desired outcomes of one kind or another (something you want but don't yet have).

In class, learning outcomes are a vision of what the children will be able to do by the end of an activity, lesson or series of lessons or after a particular input, practice or experience has happened. Obviously, the level of desire for an outcome will vary from person to person and from outcome to outcome, but if there is no desire at all then there is no desired outcome.

An important part of your craft as a teacher is to find ways for your students to be motivated because without motivation there is scant progress. When you work with a clean approach, you can facilitate children to discover and develop their own motivations. They come to learn more about themselves, what motivates them and what they are like when they are motivated. This kind of intrinsic motivation is compelling, and because the children generate it themselves, *you* don't have to expend energy maintaining it.

# Facilitating change

When you facilitate change you are no longer purely modelling something (e.g. an object, an action, a thought process) that exists in the here and now. You are using your modelling skills to explore outcomes. Outcomes are future focused.

Modelling an outcome develops a detailed and tangible sense of it, even though it exists only as a future possibility.

When goal-setting it is common to design goals, targets or outcomes to be SMART – that is specific, measurable, assignable, realistic and time-related (see Doran, 1981). Preferably, children write down their own goals in order to make their outcomes concrete, to bring them to life and to afford a sense of ownership.

Teachers usually play a part in setting SMART targets. In order to decide whether a child's goal is SMART, they must inevitably draw on their own perspectives. This can result in a child's goals becoming tweaked to match the teacher's views – often unintentionally and frequently unconsciously.

Clean facilitation differs from this. When practising clean facilitation you won't be drawing on your personal perspectives as guidance, but instead you will work with the child's own words – their description of their desired outcome. With clean facilitation children remain the authors of their own goals. You can tease out specifics and examine them in fine detail but the authority resides with the child. The deep reflection which comes about as a result of clean questioning forges a connection with the outcome and promotes a sense of ownership. Information is elicited in a way which makes it meaningful and children connect with their outcomes.

When you take a child's outcome and model it using Symbolic Modelling, that child will experience an embodied sense of it, in present time, as though they have reached into the future, grasped the experience, brought it back to the present moment and are now trying it on for size. There is nothing like it for thoroughly checking out plans – and not always, but surprisingly often, it can result in the outcome being achieved right there in the moment.

For example, in a gymnastics lesson the children were creating and performing sequences, and one of the outcomes was to perform their sequence with poise and appropriate body tension. The children indicated that they knew what was expected of them as they waited to begin – some with arms crossed, some with legs crossed and some with hips 'cocked'. They looked a motley crew! As I asked clean questions only a couple of individuals responded verbally, but the whole class responded non-verbally as they made a personal connection with the learning outcome.

This is what happened:

| Question | Verbal response | Non-verbal response |
| --- | --- | --- |
| ... and poise ... and is there anything else about poise? | Standing up straight. | |
| ... and straight ... and is there anything else about straight? | Like hanging on a string (*referring to work we had done in previous lessons*). | |
| ... and hanging on a string ... and that's like what – when you are hanging on a string like that? | It's like floating because your feet nearly don't really touch the floor ... and it's like being stretched without even making yourself. | |
| Oh ... OK ... (*looking around the room at all the beautifully poised gymnasts*) ... begin. | | |

They had embodied the learning outcome as the questions were asked and achieved it from their initial moves. Getting a clear or embodied sense of an outcome helps children to consider with increased specificity what needs to happen to achieve it, *before* they set out to achieve it.

Symbolic Modelling can be used in various settings. Outcomes may be initiated by the teacher, by the children or imposed (i.e. taken from the curriculum or other external sources). It is effective in any scenario where a coaching approach is appropriate (i.e. where there is a desired outcome or a person wants to make progress from A to B), and is particularly effective when you are working with attitudes and emotions. Classroom contexts include working towards learning objectives or behavioural targets, confidence-building, making friends, behaviour management, motivation, conflict management and performance improvement.

When focusing on outcomes a key question to ask is, '... and what would you like to have happen?' This question invites a child to consider their desired outcome. You will notice it's not asking them what they want to *have*, what they want to *do* or what (or how) they want to *be*. It's a question that neatly avoids specifics, leaving the choice of outcome open. When an answer arrives in the form of an outcome, you can use your clean questioning skills to develop it so the child has a rich, multisensory experience of it. (For more about recognising the form of a desired outcome and what to do if an answer is not expressed in the form of an outcome, see PRO on page 138.)

A key benefit of facilitating children with a clean approach when they are formulating outcomes is that they conceive their own outcomes, so they are a perfect fit for each individual. When children have genuine ownership like this, it's generative; determining their goals *for* them is 'an act of infantilization' (Kline, 1999: 150).

Six-year-old Joe was assessing his writing and considering what needed to happen next:

| Me: | And what would you like to have happen? |
|---|---|
| Joe: | I can't read my own writing! (*with a glum facial expression*) |
| Me: | And ... you can't read your own writing ... and when you can't read your own writing, what would you like to have happen? |
| Joe: | Well, I want to be able to read it, of course. |
| Me: | And you want to be able to read it, of course. |
| | ... and what needs to happen for you to read it? |
| Joe: | I need to not join up for a start! (*laughing*) |
| Me: | And you need to not join up ... and is there anything el ... (*Joe interrupts*) |
| Joe: | I need to leave spaces between the words. |
| Me: | And you need to leave spaces between words ... |

... and what needs to happen for you to leave spaces between the words?

Joe: I need to do my writing more smaller and then there will be more space to leave spaces between the words.

Me: And you need to do your writing more smaller ... (*he interrupts again*).

Joe: Well, just smaller. (*correcting his own grammar*)

Me: Just smaller ... and is there anything else that needs to happen?

Joe: No.

Me: And smaller writing ... and spaces between words ... and read your own writing ... hmm ... and smaller writing ... can that happen?

(*There is a long pause as he scans his writing, looking intently*)

Joe: Yee ... es.

Me: And spaces between words ... can that happen?

Joe: Yes!

Joe strode back to his desk enthusiastically and set about his writing, confident in the next steps he had decided he needed to take.

Of course, I could have just told him to make his writing smaller and to leave spaces between words, but he wouldn't have had such a sense of ownership, he wouldn't have thought it through so carefully (what you can't see from the transcript is the intensity with which he scanned the text and the depth of consideration that went into his planning decision), neither of us would have picked up on his need to temporarily stop focusing on 'joining up' (which was leading to overload and frustration) and he certainly wouldn't have generated such a skip in his stride and a commitment to practice. And he hadn't just worked out the next step in his handwriting progression, he had begun to learn how to devise his own next steps in any learning pursuit, independently.

# Considering necessary conditions

Having elicited and developed an outcome, the next step is to find out what needs to happen to achieve it. Sometimes, as illustrated earlier in the gymnastics example, just developing the outcome is enough for a child to achieve it, but normally there are conditions that need to be met (e.g. obstacles to be overcome, resources to tap into, other people to consider) before the goal can be achieved. Key questions to ask are:

- ... and what needs to happen for (desired outcome)?

- ... and what needs to happen for (desired outcome) to happen?

- ... and is there anything else that needs to happen for (desired outcome)?

When I asked Joe, 'And what needs to happen for you to leave spaces between the words?' he realised there would be no room in the text box on the page to leave spaces between words unless he reduced the size of his writing. Taking a second or two to realise this probably saved him a couple of frustrating false starts and in the long run saved time on the task. If I had told him to reduce the size of his writing I would have robbed him of an experience that boosted his capacity to take his own learning forward – and he would not have gained such confidence.

Joe could see that in order to achieve his outcome (to be able to read his own writing) he needed to do two small things: to 'not join up' and to leave spaces between words. On the face of it they are both minor changes but there were still conditions that needed to be met. I didn't ask about the 'not join up' so it's not clear if there were conditions for this, but I did ask about the 'leave spaces between words' and we discovered one further condition – to write 'more smaller'.

Joe's outcome was a baby step. Some outcomes are more like giant strides in comparison and they often have more conditions – and sometimes there may be conditions for those conditions. It's important to deal with all of them to avoid potential barriers to progress. It's also important to identify which condition needs to be satisfied first. Often, achieving the first condition can (surprisingly for the child) make the rest of the conditions easier or even redundant, as you can see in the example of Jenny below.

Nine-year-old Jenny's desired outcome was to speak confidently in assembly. The two conditions that needed to be met for her to achieve this were to know her words by heart and to be able to speak up.

I asked her: 'And can you "know words by heart"?' She replied: 'Well, I can know them off by heart but then, when I get nervous, I go and forget them, which can be a bit embarrassing really.' I asked: 'And what needs to happen for "know words by heart"?' She considered for a moment or two and concluded that she would need to focus on the 'heart of the message' rather than on memorising individual words. When she was clear about the heart of the message then she would 'know words by heart'. When she focused on the heart of the message, although 'nervous' was still present, it was in the background of her attention and no longer presented as a problem. Once it was no longer a problem, she was able to speak up with confidence.

Two other key questions are:

- ... and can you (necessary condition)?
- ... and can (necessary condition)?

The 'can you (...)?' or 'can (...)?' question checks out whether the child considers it achievable or if there are prior conditions which need to be met before there can be movement towards the outcome. When they reflect on 'what needs to happen?' and 'can that happen?', and if there is 'anything else that needs to happen?' and 'can that happen?', they will have considered all the factors they need to in order to address an outcome.

# Monitoring progress

A child's view of what is achievable may be different to yours, of course. When they put their ideas into action they will find out from the feedback (from the real world) whether their assessment of 'achievability' is accurate or if it needs to be adjusted. Penny Tompkins and James Lawley call this the 'trial and feedback' method of learning. It's extremely effective in developing independent learning skills.

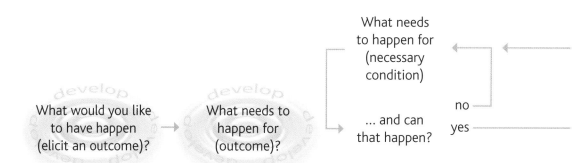

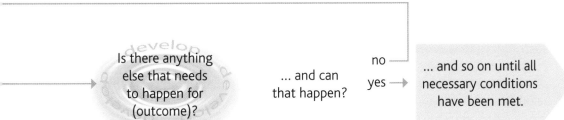

# What happens when children can have what they want?

For most children, considering what they would like to have happen and then whether that can indeed happen is a fairly straightforward process. For some children, it's only when they realise that they can have what they want that they are able to consider whether they actually want it. Many are so accustomed to asking (or silently wishing) and not getting that they stop considering exactly what it is they are asking for – and/or the genuine possibility of getting it comes as a shock to them.

Other children, having asked for what they want are 'corrected' or 'influenced' by the adults around them to want something else instead. After a while these children learn to want what they predict the adult wants them to want, and in time they lose touch with their own desires. Marketing messages and peer pressure can affect them similarly. With these individuals you will need to work with patience.

No doubt you will have come across some children who are out to avoid tasks altogether. It's surprisingly easy for their behaviour to be misinterpreted as lazy, disruptive, disaffected or as an inability to understand. When all necessary conditions are addressed as described above, it's often only then that the real issues surface and the child recognises them and can address them – for instance, fear of success, fear of failure or shame. In such circumstances the clean questions come into their own, with the caveat again to 'tread softly'.

# What happens when children can't have what they want?

It's all well and good asking children what they would like to have happen, but what if they say, 'I want to play all day' or 'I want to skip the writing'? A school environment isn't conducive to children having exactly what they want, moment by moment. The system isn't geared that way. There are other people to consider, there are rules to be adhered to and there is the curriculum, of course. Balancing the constraints of society with individual desires is an important life skill.

If children don't encounter boundaries (for whatever reason, perhaps because they are cosseted or disregarded) they miss out on important life lessons. They don't learn the resilience to be OK with the pain of not getting what they want, the persistence to try again in a different way, the appreciation that sometimes other people's needs are more important or the recognition that it may not be appropriate for their wants to be met there and then (or at all). So how can this be reconciled with children tailoring their own outcomes?

# Framing outcomes

I use a framing statement to set contexts and boundaries. There are some examples below. You can adapt the pattern of the framing statement, tailoring it to specific circumstances by replacing the words in italics to suit each situation, as it occurs, in your classroom. Be sure to emphasise the emboldened '**and**' each time.

> And you want to *chat with Jane* now and *Jane can't chat* because she needs to finish her work. And when you want to *chat with Jane* **and** *Jane can't chat*, what would you like to have happen?

> And you want to *chat with Jane* now and *you have to finish your writing* before you can go out to play. And when you want to *chat with Jane* **and** *you have to finish your writing*, what would you like to have happen?

> And you want to *chat with Jane* now and *we've all agreed to work in silence* to support the people who are taking exams. And when you want to *chat with Jane* **and** *we've all agreed to work in silence*, what would you like to have happen?

In these circumstances, the question sometimes needs to be asked a few times before the child fully realises what is being asked of them. Once that realisation takes place the focus of the conversation shifts. The question acknowledges the child's desire and communicates the reality that their desire can't happen or that it can't happen as they would like. Once that reality is appreciated, the question shifts attention from the original want to a new want (a new outcome).

When children can't have what they want, and you acknowledge it like this, their wants are validated and they learn invaluable lessons: that it's OK to want anything but that it's not OK to expect every want to be satisfied and that it's not OK to act on every want.

# How do you put the principles we've been discussing into action in a busy classroom?

In 2002, Penny Tompkins and James Lawley developed a beautifully simple framework which I have adapted for use as a support when asking the questions in a classroom context or when working one-to-one. The series of 'crib cards' – which are small enough to tuck into my pocket (stuck back to back in pairs to produce five cards in all) – helped me to hold the framework in mind when responding in the moment and to keep my bearings. (To read an example of this in action, see Chapter 9.)

**1. Elicit a desired outcome**

- What would you like to have happen?

**2. Develop the desired outcome**

- And is there anything else about (...)?
- And what kind of (...)?
- And where is (...)?
- And whereabouts is (...)?

**3. Elicit a metaphor**

- And that's (child's words – optional) like what?

Note: If a metaphor for their outcome emerges, go on to develop it using the developing questions overleaf.

**4. Develop a metaphor**

- And is there anything else about (...)?
- And what kind of (...)?
- And where is (...)?
- And whereabouts is (...)?

## 5. Elicit the first of any necessary conditions

- And what needs to happen for (desired outcome)?

## 6. Develop the first of any necessary conditions

- And is there anything else about (necessary condition)?

Note: The intention of this question is to find out more about the necessary condition, but you don't need to find out more unless you think it has the potential to enhance clarity. In most cases, just knowing that a particular necessary condition exists is liberating for a person – it means they can consider their options – so you'll only use this question occasionally.

## 7. Elicit any other necessary conditions (if any more exist)

- And is there anything else that needs to happen for (desired outcome)?

## 8. Develop any other necessary conditions (if any more exist)

- And is there anything else about (necessary condition)?

Note: If another necessary condition does exist, then treat it in the same way as the first.

## 9. Mature any changes

- And is there anything else about (...)?

- And what kind of (...)?

- And where is (...)?

Note: If at any point you notice changes in metaphors or in conceptual descriptions, use developing questions to flesh out the new details.

- And whereabouts is (...)?'

## 10. And then what happens?

- This is a useful question to ask to explore the effects of a desired outcome and the effects of a condition and to mature a change.

## Assessment for learning

When learning outcomes are made clear and success criteria identified and agreed by the children, they are able to monitor their progress towards the established outcomes. The crib cards (modified by removing the metaphor stages 3 and 4) offer a useful scaffold to support children as they generate their own success criteria – although, even if the metaphor stage is removed, children will still talk in metaphor, as in the 'learn by heart' example above. They can be used to support reflective thinking as children assess their own progress, considering their work against the success criteria for self or peer monitoring.

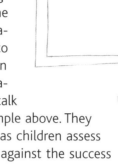

## The problem with problem-solving

Having a model like this works well when outcomes are clear, but clear outcomes are not always easy to formulate. Children often focus on recounting their problems, or on working out how to remedy them, rather than focusing on what they actually want and how they can bring that about.

Robert Fritz (1989) explains that because human beings are creatures of habit, and because we tend to take the path of least resistance, we tackle problems or conflicts by devising solutions to get rid of them – going from problem to problem and devising solution after solution. This results in an oscillating pattern: problem–solution–problem–solution. An example of an oscillating pattern in the school context is where a particular playground game is banned to eradicate dangerous behaviour and although there are short-term improvements, before long the children have invented another, equally unacceptable, game to play.

This is fundamentally different from the process of creating which brings outcomes into being. Like drawing back the string of a bow or stretching an elastic band, we can generate sustainable momentum towards our outcomes by focusing our attention on our outcome and also on our current reality, to create what

Fritz calls 'structural tension' (Fritz, 1991). And because 'tension seeks resolution', motivating energy is generated (as in the diagram below).

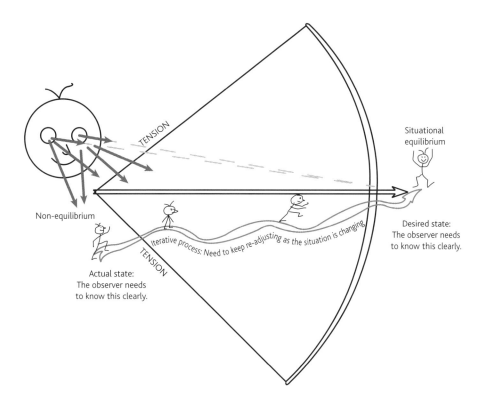

When you foster an outcome focus with the children in your class you are cultivating the process of creating. So how do you direct children's attention to outcomes? First, you need to be able to distinguish between a problem, a remedy and an outcome. James Lawley and Penny Tompkins developed a model to help distinguish between them called the PRO model:

- Problems are expressions of what is wrong, what is not liked. They contain no desire for change. They don't specify an outcome.

- Remedies are expressions of what is not wanted. They are ways of getting rid of or reducing a problem. They don't say what it will be like once the problem is solved.

- Outcomes are expressions of what is wanted. They are expressions of a desire to add something of benefit (something more or better than the current reality).

When you hold this model in mind as you are listening, you can identify whether a pupil is expressing a problem, a remedy for a problem or an outcome (you will recall that you made a start on listening with this kind of discrimination in Chapter 2 in the task for week 5).

Here are some examples:

| Problem | Remedy | Desired outcome |
| --- | --- | --- |
| I don't understand his long-winded explanations. | I'd prefer less of the detail. | I want to understand more about this subject. |
| I'm worried about sleepless nights in the lead-up to the lesson observation. | I have to be less nervous before lesson observations. | I feel confident about my lesson observation. |
| I can't stop them chattering. | I want to get rid of the constant low-level interruptions. | I generate more of a learning atmosphere – a buzz – in the classroom. |
| I don't want to spend hours each night slaving away at lesson plans, thank you very much. | I need to be able to create great lesson plans in less time and with less effort. | I'm inspired with great ideas and my planning slips easily into my schedule. |

| Nobody will play with me. | I want them to stop leaving me out. | I want more friends. |
|---|---|---|
| I hate reading. | I wish the words were easier. | I like reading – it's fun. |
| I'm scared I'll forget my words in the class play. | I want to write the words on cue cards, so I don't have to worry so much. | I say my words confidently. |
| They keep talking all the time. | I need them to be quieter. | I can concentrate and get on with my work. |

Once you are able to distinguish between a problem, a remedy and an outcome you can use the PRO model to direct children's attention towards their outcomes.

# Directing attention to outcomes

- When a child expresses a *problem* you can help them move their attention to an outcome focus by asking, 'And when ... (parrot-phrase their problem statement), what would you like to have happen?'

- When a child expresses a *remedy* you can help move their attention to an outcome focus by asking a question, but in this instance don't parrot-phrase but repeat back their remedy statement, altering the tense as though the remedy has been achieved, and remove the 'wanting words' (e.g. 'And when ... (rephrased future-tense remedy statement without the wanting words), then what happens?').

- When a child expresses an *outcome* you ask, 'And when ... (parrot-phrase their outcome), is there anything else about (selected part of their outcome)?' Then go on to develop their outcome in the usual way (see Chapter 2).

| Examples of wanting words/phrases in common use | | | | | |
|---|---|---|---|---|---|
| want | wish | hope | look for | aspire | crave |
| lust after | yearn | heart set on | need | require | could do with |
| fancy | feel like | desire | would like | long for | hanker after |

When you leave out the wanting words, look what happens:

| Remedy statement with wanting words highlighted | Rephrased future-tense remedy with wanting words removed |
|---|---|
| *I'd prefer to* have less of the detail. | And when you have less of the detail, then what happens? |
| *I have to* be less nervous before lesson observations. | And when you are less nervous before lesson observations, then what happens? |
| *I want to* get rid of the constant low-level interruptions. | And when you get rid of the constant low-level interruptions, then what happens? |
| *I need to* be able to create great lesson plans in less time and with less effort. | And when you are able to create great lesson plans in less time and with less effort, then what happens? |
| *I want them* to stop leaving me out. | And when they stop leaving you out, then what happens? |
| *I wish* the words were easier. | And when the words are easier, then what happens? |

| Remedy statement with wanting words highlighted | Rephrased future-tense remedy with wanting words removed |
|---|---|
| *I want* the words on cue cards, so I don't have to worry so much. | And when the words are on cue cards and you don't worry so much, then what happens? |
| *I need* them to be quiet. | And when they are quiet, then what happens? |

You can see in these examples that the perspective shifts to a place in time beyond the remedy – to *after* it's happened. From this perspective (where there are no obstacles to their outcomes) the person is free to consider what they would like to have happen, so attention can now be focused fully on the outcome. Sometimes though (surprisingly often in fact) the person will create another remedy rather than focus on their outcome.

When this happens, just respond as before asking, 'And when ... (reformulating their remedy with an altered tense and the wanting word removed), then what happens?' and cycle through this as many times as the person creates remedies until they finally arrive at an outcome. It's worth emphasising here that it can take patience and tenacity. Remember, it's not as common for people to know their outcomes as it is for them to know their problems and their remedies. For example:

| Problem | Nobody will play with me. |
|---|---|
| Response | And when nobody will play with you, what would you like to have happen? |
| Problem | They all leave me out. |
| Response | And when they all leave you out, what would you like to have happen? |

| Problem | They keep running away from me. | | |
|---|---|---|---|
| Response | And when they keep running away from you, what would you like to have happen? | | |
| Remedy | I want them to stop leaving me out. | | |
| Response | And when they stop leaving you out, then what happens? | | |
| Remedy | I feel less lonely. | | |
| Response | And when you feel less lonely, then what happens? | | |
| Remedy | I don't feel so left out. | | |
| Response | And when you don't feel so left out, then what happens? | | |
| Outcomes (a selection) | I can join in with them. | I make friends with them. | I feel happy. |
| Responses (a selection) | And you can join in with them … and when *join in* … is there anything else about *join in*? | And you make friends with them … and when you *make friends* … is there anything else about *make, when you make friends*? | And you feel happy … and when *you feel happy* … what kind of *happy*? |
| Developing outcomes | I can run around with them and then, if I get tagged, I'll be it and then I will be playing with them. | Well, I'll do the asking instead of just waiting for them to ask me. | Happy that I can go and ask them. Happy that I'm confident enough to ask them. |

# Why bother?

Some teachers are nervous about asking children what they would like to have happen in case they become demanding or anarchic. In my experience, in mainstream education, this doesn't happen. When children are offered moments (and supported) to reflect on what they want, they find that they want something in sync with their setting, something sociable and acceptable.

When they know they have been heard, children become less demanding and more able to make adjustments and compromise. When working with a clean approach in whole-class settings, children become more aware of each other's sensibilities and needs, and this enhances respect and consideration among the group.

Jeff would jump around the classroom. His behaviour disrupted lessons and he often had to miss playtime as a consequence. He hated this and was constantly angry as a result. It was a vicious circle. When he stopped to consider what he would like to have happen, with the support of clean questioning, he realised he wanted to be thinking on his feet (he needed to move to be learning at his best). The rest of the class respected this, and he respected their needs by pacing and jumping around in a corner of the room out of their way. Lessons went smoothly and the quality and quantity of his work improved.

The children in a low-achieving spelling group moved beyond, 'Don't care!', 'I can't' and 'too scared to try' as they realised that, if possible, they would like to be able to spell well. They began to support each other's learning needs and their previous avoidance behaviour transformed into self-motivation and independent learning.

Once Steve had reflected on his outcome, he realised he didn't want to be mean to Katie (see page 239).

It's a rare and valuable experience for us to take time to consider what we want. When you facilitate this in your classroom, what you are offering is priceless.

## Practice task

- Work on a desired outcome using the crib cards on pages 134–135.

- Distinguish between problem, remedy and outcome statements and ask yourself appropriate questions to arrive at a desired outcome.

- Ask questions about the outcome statements.

- Practise on different outcomes until you are confident with the process.

- When you are confident, work one-to-one with a child, friend or colleague.

- When you are familiar with the framework, the questions and reformulating statements, begin to practise in whole-class situations focusing on, for example, learning objectives and success criteria (e.g. facilitating the class to generate the learning objective (moving the focus from problem to remedy to outcome if appropriate) and identifying any necessary conditions (which usually translate into success criteria)).

As teachers, we are constantly aiming to facilitate pupil progress towards one outcome or another (and for ourselves, with regard to professional development), but taking account of the strengths and needs of a diverse group of children in a range of curriculum areas can be a major challenge. With the clean approaches you have encountered thus far, you will be able to facilitate change from moment to moment, responding to individuals with masterful flexibility, supporting them at their learning edge and facilitating them to move beyond it with a few well-placed questions.

# Part 2
# Applying Clean Language in the Classroom

# Chapter 7
# Laying the Foundations

## One-to-one

### Short conversations

At the start of a new year I introduce clean questions informally to the children through everyday one-to-one conversations. I don't talk about them, I just use them informally during the course of the day whenever it seems appropriate – which is often.

This means the children become familiar with hearing and answering the questions well before we ever talk about them or think about using them as a learning tool. In a mixed year group class, some of the children may have already spent a year familiarising themselves with the questions, so this serves as a comfortable reminder for them as they ease their way back into the new school year.

For example, when a child shows me his teddy in class, I might say, '… and what kind of teddy is that?' or '… and is there anything else about that teddy?' I ask the questions in a conversational style, which is speedier and more natural than the full syntax (see page 57). As children nearby overhear these conversations, they are also experiencing the questioning process in a low-key, informal and natural way.

When children are learning particularly effectively in class, I draw attention to it, perhaps by describing it:

> I can see you have collected a lot of information there.
>
> I can see you are trying different ways of calculating that.
>
> I hear you are explaining clearly to your partner now – point by point.
>
> I hear you reading that with a lovely natural expression now.

Or sometimes I'll ask a few questions about it:

> Good learning … and when you are learning like that … what's that like?
>
> Great learning … and what's that like for you?

Later, when the children have become used to reflecting on their learning state like this, I might deliver the question in this form:

What are you like when you are learning like that?

Later still it will become:

And when you're learning at your best ... you are (or it's) ... like ... what?

However, it's not the exactness of the question that matters, it's the effect the question has on the child, it's where their attention goes in response to the question. But be aware that although slight variations make little or no difference, every added word increases the likelihood that the questioner has an agenda – attempting to lead the child to an answer rather than aiming for the child to find out something for themselves.

In the playground, when children are hurt, angry or upset, I use clean questions to help them resolve their difficulties because it saves a lot of time and is more likely to result in outcomes that satisfy the individuals involved. Because the children devise the outcomes themselves, they have genuine ownership of them (for some examples see Chapter 9).

When children are talking about their feelings, I invite them to attend to their own experience by asking a few clean questions. For instance, if a child says, 'I'm really happy', I might reply with one of these responses:

Happy ... and is there anything else about that?

Happy ... and what kind of happy?

Ah, happy ... and whereabouts is that happy?

In this way, children begin to discover more about the qualities of their feelings *and* that feelings have a location (see page 50–52). These informal moments happen spontaneously and are usually brief, lasting only seconds or a few minutes at most.

## Longer conversations

Sometimes I'll use Clean Language in slightly longer conversations with individuals – for instance, when a child is focusing on an outcome or they want something to change. This can happen naturally if you are working in a one-to-one session.

In the following example a child wanted to change what was happening at home with her reading practice. Whenever she came upon a difficult or unknown word in a passage and managed to work it out, her dad would pat her on the head in congratulation. This was uncomfortable for her, so she did what she could to avoid reading at home.

As she came to an unknown word in a passage she was reading to me, our conversation began spontaneously as she told me about her problem:

| | |
|---|---|
| Me: | … and what would you like to have happen … when you don't know a word like that? |
| Child: | For daddy to whisper it in my ear. |
| Me: | … and you'd like daddy to whisper it in your ear. And when you don't know a word, and when daddy whispers it in your ear, then what happens? |
| Child: | It makes me feel like I can actually read the hard words. |
| Me: | … and when you feel you can actually read the hard words …? |
| Child: | (*interrupting*) It gives me a little tinkle in my neck. |
| Me: | Oh … and it gives you a little tinkle in your neck … and what kind of tinkle? |
| Child: | It's just like a little shiny tinkly star in my neck. |
| Me: | Ah … and whereabouts little shiny tinkly …? |
| Child: | It's in the middle. Right here in the middle. And then it goes like a hundred little spiky stars around my neck. |
| Me: | Oh … a hundred little spiky stars? |
| Child: | Yes, all holding hands in a circle, flashing … moving around in a circle. They're moving … flashing around my neck. Then they move the other way. |

Me:     ... and when flashing little stars, around your neck ... all holding hands and moving around in a circle ... and the other way (*pointing*), what happens to reading?

Child:  It makes me feel a little bit better and I can read those actually hard words.

Me:     ... and it makes you feel a little bit better and you can read those actually hard words. And ... what needs to happen for that to happen?

Child:  I can ask him to stop patting me on the head when I do it well ... and he can give me a kiss on the head after I have read a whole sentence.

Me:     ... and you can ask him to stop patting you on the head when you do it well and ... he can give you a kiss on the head after you have read a whole sentence.

Child:  I can ask him that as well.

Me:     ... and is there anything else about that?

Child:  No. I can ask him.

She'd had an embodied experience of what it's like for her when she's reading well, and she had worked out what she wanted her dad to do in response to her good reading instead of patting her on the head. Later in the day she asked me to write a note in her reading diary (a diary for communication between home and school) to say that she had thought of a new way to do reading at home and wanted to share it with her dad.

She went on to coach her dad on how best to support her reading. She was also able to explain to him how he could best help her with difficult words, and the best time, place and ambience for her reading practice. Once she had engaged with her needs and felt able to assert them, she no longer had to be encouraged and cajoled to read – she began to take up the running herself.

# Working with the whole class

## Joyful imaginings

During the settling in period at the beginning of the year, I also introduce the children to what the infants call 'joyful imaginings' and the juniors call 'imagineering'. The children and I (and any other willing adults) lie down and relax for a few minutes each day on child-sized fluffy blankets while they listen to a story from a Relax Kids CD (www.relaxkids.com).

The children close their eyes and become still and relaxed as they imagine themselves floating on a magic carpet or sliding down a rainbow. This multi-sensory visualisation lasts just three minutes. Children find a place away from distractions and lie down on their blankets pretty quickly so they don't miss a second of it.

For the first few weeks a good proportion of the class wiggle, giggle, itch and scratch as they lie listening. In time (you need to be patient enough to wait for it) the children begin to settle into relaxation and lose themselves to their imaginations. Following these sessions they move quietly to their desks and remain silent as they draw what they have imagined.

When the children have finished their drawings they share them with each other. They are usually surprised when they see how other children's interpretations of the story are different from their own. As they talk to each other I mingle, asking individuals clean questions about elements of their drawings.

Me:      Tell me about your drawing.

Child:    It's a rainbow slide with a mat like a raindrop.

Me:      Ah ... it's a rainbow slide with a mat like a raindrop ...

          ... and raindrop

          ... and is there anything else about that raindrop?

This invariably elicits more detail about both what the child has imagined and their drawing, and again the questioning process itself serves as a model. When the time is right I ask clean questions of the whole class about their drawings. How do I know when the time is right? When the children are responding confidently to questions during the informal one-to-one sessions and in group/whole-class 'show and tell' sessions, I know I can ask about their drawings and they will be able to respond with ease.

How do I ask about 30 different drawings at the same time? I ask the children to identify an element in their drawing, 'Choose "something" in your drawing and put your finger on it ...', and then ask:

    ... and what kind of thing (or 'something') is that thing (or 'something')?

    ... tell your talk-partner.

    ... and is there anything else about that thing (or 'something')?

    ... tell your talk-partner.

As the children talk to each other about their drawings they often become aware of additional detail, which they can add to their drawings then and there.

The next step is for the children to begin to use the questions themselves. They might do this in pairs or in small groups. One group member will show their picture and the others will ask questions (any questions at first). When they are familiar with the activity, I introduce the clean questions and invite the children to use them themselves. Because they have already heard me using the questions in other contexts, it's not a big deal for them. Some will already have begun to use them spontaneously in response to the informal modelling and others will begin to use them now.

# Show and tell

Alongside the other activities in the first few weeks of term, I'll begin to use clean questions in show and tell sessions (with older children this happens in any open class discussion). When a child brings an object or a newsworthy subject to show and talk about, their classmates ask questions about it. For example, a child may show his teddy, and when the questioning begins, it goes something like this:

> Did your mummy buy it?
>
> Yes.
>
> Do you like it?
>
> Yes.

These questions are not just closed; in many cases the child asking the question already knows the answer (children rarely bring in something they dislike). During the questioning I draw children's attention to the effects of the questions and some children are able to see that some questions draw out more information from the listener than others.

I demonstrate both open and closed questions and we compare the responses to them. Once the children know about open and closed questions, if a child delivers a closed question, such as 'Did your mummy buy that?', I'll say, 'Whoa ... stop for a moment ... what do you think their answer will be?' Most children are able to predict that the answer will be 'Yes' or 'No', and soon they are experts at spotting closed questions.

Once a reasonable proportion of the class can see the difference between open and closed questions, and they have got the hang of asking open ones, I wait my turn before using a series of clean questions which focus attention on one attribute of the object on show (or the subject of the talk). The series is usually made up of, 'And is there anything else about (...)?' and 'And what kind of (...)?'

The children soon begin to take on this technique themselves. Once they are using them confidently I'll ask them, 'What does that question do?' This question usually generates a lot of discussion and often the children notice that the clean questions they have been asking elicit further information and make people think. In time, and with plenty of experience of using them, even quite young children (from around the age of 7) are able to reflect on the effect of the questions.

---

## Practice tips

- Rather than classifying questions in terms of their description (open/ closed or clean/leading), think of them in terms of their effects on the mind of the listener.

- Notice how the questions act on the attention or perception of the listener – how they widen, broaden, open up or narrow, close down, focus.

---

With a limited palette of clean questions, children are soon able to choose and deliver an appropriate question, attend to the response and then choose another question to direct a partner's attention to a further aspect of the subject. This can be particularly satisfying for them. We continue in this manner for a week or so while they become familiar with the questions and with asking them. The children work together as a team, chipping in and helping each other as they go (see pages 85–87).

With the questioning happening in such a variety of contexts throughout the day, over the course of a few weeks the children gain experience of answering and asking clean questions and listening carefully to responses, so they become familiar with them. They meet with the questions unobtrusively, little and often, every day.

# Using the questions in lessons

After a while the children are so familiar with the questions that, as I begin to ask one, they will second guess it and ask it themselves. When this happens (about two or three weeks after the start of term), I know the children are ready to explore the functions of the questions.

The children work in pairs. They examine pictures, taking it in turns to point at objects in the pictures and ask questions about them. This exercise is usually linked to work in other subjects (i.e. art, literacy, PSHE or 'joyful imaginings'). For example:

What's that?

It's a bridge.

And is there anything else about bridge?

It's a wooden bridge.

And what kind of wooden bridge?

One that's in a garden. That goes over a lake full of water lilies.

The pairs share what they have noticed about the pictures, and about the effects of the questions, in whole-class mini plenaries. At the end of the lesson we reflect on the session together and they tell me what they have noticed.

## Playing with the questions

Another way for children to get the hang of asking the questions, become comfortable with using them and remember them is through humour. In one class a child said, 'You can use them for anything.' And this set off a whole stream of ideas. The children laughed and giggled as they fooled around with the question, 'What kind of?'

If you were a chef, you could ask, what kind of egg? What kind of butter?

If you were an engineer, you'd say, what kind of bridge?

# A tool for independent learning

Once the children are comfortable with the questions, they can use them independently and with peers as a tool for learning in most, if not all, lessons. You can see how the children and I have used them in various curriculum areas in the rest of Part 2.

# Detail detectives

Some years ago, when the children in a class had been using the questions long enough to be well aware of the benefits, they noticed that they were constantly describing the questions in terms of their power to elicit detail. In one class a child said, 'They are like the questions a detective might use.' From then on we began to call them detail detective questions because it described the function of the questions in a way that made sense to them. The children think of themselves as detail detectives, and clean questions have become detail detective questions or DDQs. Children warm to the idea of being a detective and they easily understand the role of the questions through this metaphor.

Children enjoy directing attention using a mock magnifying glass (after Sherlock Holmes) as a visual reminder of the questions and their purpose. The DDQ magnifying glass (see Appendix B) displays clean questions around the rim so the children can refer to them as they observe the subject of their questions through the lens. On one side are the developing questions. Turn it over and you will find the sequence questions (... and then what happens? ... and what happens next?). They appear on the reverse because turning the magnifying glass over serves as a reminder for the children that they are switching from detecting the spatial aspects of a subject and the form to detecting a sequence (moving forward or back in time).

Children also enjoy spotting moments in class when the DDQs will help. They say, 'I think we need some detail detective questions, Miss,' or, 'Hey, cue the DDQs!' When children are using the magnifying glasses confidently they become an everyday learning tool. Later, when they have internalised the questions, they can work without the magnifying glasses. Children also like to use DDQ fans or DDQ dice (see Appendices D and E). Both can be used as an alternative to the magnifying glass, to practise saying or selecting questions to ask and to draw attention to the function of the questions.

# Whole-class learning culture

Having introduced the questions and provided opportunities for the children to become familiar with them (as described above), the next step is to use them to develop a whole-class learning culture. We have already seen (in Chapter 4) how individual learning metaphors can be developed and used to create shared metaphors for the whole-class environment and to support a collaborative, learning culture.

> ## Practice task
>
> Reread the section on developing a learning metaphor for the classroom if necessary (see page 76).
>
> Then ... have a go yourself!

# Chapter 8
# Making a Meal of Spellings

## Spelling with sausages

One of the first recipients of my new Clean Language skills was a 10-year-old who I'll call Annabel. Annabel was in Year 6 and couldn't spell. Annabel, her parents and staff at her school were becoming increasingly concerned. She was approximately two years behind. Interventions over the years had resulted in meagre progress and now secondary school was looming, so the special needs coordinator asked if there was anything I could do to help. Annabel was an intelligent and capable child with high levels of attainment in all areas except spelling. As I knew she was successful in other areas, I figured it might be a good idea to begin by exploring some of her strengths.

We met while the rest of the school were having assembly. I asked Annabel where she would like to be. At first she was puzzled – children are accustomed to being told whether to sit or stand, and where to sit and so on, so this was something new for her. Asking children where *they* would like to be sends a message right from the start that the locus of control is with them.

Annabel chose a place in the school where she was comfortable to work and we began. She told me about some of the things she enjoyed and what she could do well. She described what it was like for her when she was doing them and I encouraged her to describe in as much sensory detail as she could. I asked her to describe both external sensory input (what she could hear, see, feel, smell and taste around her) and internal perceptions (what she could see in her mind's eye, hear, feel, taste and smell internally).

As Annabel described her experiences, I asked questions that focused her attention with more precision – questions like, 'What kind of feeling?', 'Whereabouts is it?' and 'Is there anything else about that?' Annabel's answers helped me to develop a better sense of her experience and finding answers to the questions helped her to notice more about her own experience, so she developed a better sense of it as well. We were both forming an increasingly detailed idea of what it was like for her when she was doing something well.

So often in the past, when working with difficulties, I would focus on the problems – on what the child couldn't do – and I would devise activities to overcome those difficulties. Today we focused on what was already working well – we began to model Annabel's resourceful state. She said that when she was doing something particularly well it was like 'fizzing and bubbling'. This was located in her belly and rose up through her body. It was inside, directly in the middle, and 'strenuous' like popping candy. As Annabel described fizzing and bubbling rising up, I watched her posture change – she stood taller and began to smile. Her gaze changed too. Previously she had been glancing down with her line of sight flicking from right to left close to her body. Now she was standing tall and looking ahead with a beaming smile and twinkle in her eye.

I wanted to make best use of the time available but having made such a good start, I wasn't sure what to do next. I felt a little lost at sea, so thinking on my feet, I trusted in Annabel to know what needed to happen and asked her. While she was in (what I interpreted to be) a resourceful state, I asked her what she would like to have happen next. She said she wanted to be able to spell the word 'went' and get it right in a spelling test.

She explained that she had been trying in vain to spell this word for six years. She had never been able to get it right in a test and was determined to be able to spell it now. It's hard to imagine how frustrating it must have been for her. This was one of the first words she had been given to learn when she started school aged 4. All her friends had learned it quickly and easily. It's a common word and she found herself needing to use it in her writing – and having to ask how to spell it – over and over again. She was acutely aware that even children who couldn't remember how to spell it could work it out for themselves by sounding it out. She was annoyed, frustrated and ashamed that she hadn't been able to learn it in all that time. She was sensitive to the reactions of her peers, self-conscious about them witnessing some of the difficulties she was having in front of them and unwilling to receive help directly from the teaching assistant because of these anxieties.

Having considered what she wanted to have happen, I asked Annabel, 'What needs to happen for that to happen?' With the support of a few clean questions to facilitate her thinking, she went on to devise some uniquely tailored next steps for herself. So what needed to happen?

Annabel's first idea was to make the word out of plasticine, which she did. Then she decided to make it outside of her field of vision so she hid her hands underneath the table as she made it (all the while fizzing and bubbling), before placing it on the table to check it against a written example. Annabel went on to devise more novel approaches that made sense to her and appealed to her own sensory preferences. For the word 'friend', for instance, she linked the 'fizzing and bubbling popping candy' process with the idea of making 3D letters and decided that she could have both if she were to cook the word in a frying pan while singing a song. This made sense to her because 'friend' begins with 'fri' (like fry) and ends with 'end' (fri-end). So she went ahead and made the word out of sausages and fried them while singing … and then she ate them!

And to my great surprise she was able to spell both words correctly in her next spelling test. This was a turning point for Annabel because she could now see that success was possible. She had a strategy, new confidence and hope which would see her through the challenges education posed for her. It also helped her to cope with the peer pressure she was experiencing.

Seven years on, Annabel continues to use mnemonics for simple words like 'because', 'Wednesday' and 'their' and spelling is not her strength. But it's no longer holding her back and spelling assessment scores are now average for her age. Annabel completed her GCSEs achieving four A*'s, five A's (which included English literature and English language), a B in German and a C in French and went on to achieve three A's and a B at A level. Having been successful in the rigorous interview process at her chosen medical school, she has now successfully completed her first year of a medical degree (MBBS) at St George's, University of London. Annabel's mother, Christine, maintains that 'the clean intervention helped her adopt the resourceful approach which has underscored her success'.

At times, during that coaching intervention, I was tempted to take the lead with Annabel and make suggestions, but I refrained — choosing to remain clean and trust that Annabel had the resources she needed and to trust the process, despite my insecurities. The changes that began with the creation of those unusual strategies have had positive long-term effects for her. Annabel still remembers 'eating her words' with fondness as she embarks on her next exciting step. She said, 'It changed everything for me. It helped me think very differently about things.'

# Chapter 9
# Behaviour

Children should have the right to say what they think should happen, when adults are making decisions that affect them, and to have their opinions taken into account.

UN Convention on the Rights of the Child (1989)

## Clean Language in the playground

I've spent a good many years dealing with varying degrees of conflict between children in playgrounds, and I witness other adults spending a good part of their time in school working through conflict issues with children too. It's common to feel that you haven't got to the heart of it and it's not fully settled for the children.

You probably recognise the scenario … You listen to them and try to get them to appreciate each other's perspective and, 20 minutes later, after grudging apologies have been made, you are left with an uneasy sense that the issue is not resolved. But breaktime ends and lessons beckon so you bring it to a close and move on. Sometimes the children involved are able to forgive and forget within the time available, but more often than not they harbour grudges and resentments, and this can spill out later and the whole cycle starts again. This pattern can be repetitive. A huge amount of time can be eaten up by cycles of conflict and (apparent) resolution.

Used flexibly, Clean Language can cut through difficulties and clear up conflicts satisfactorily without the lingering resentments and in much less time. When children become familiar with the process they often begin to use it themselves to resolve their own friendship issues independently.

| Conflict resolution in a nutshell | |
|---|---|
| Step 1 | Ask '... and what just happened?' <br><br> Often, as in the example that follows (Star Wars and Light Sabers), children tell you what just happened without you actually asking a question. |
| Step 2 | Ask '... and what would you like to have happen?' <br><br> Often children will repeat their problem in which case you repeat your question. |
| Step 3 | Sometimes children will tell you a remedy to the problem (e.g. 'I want them to stop chasing me') instead of what they want to have happen (e.g. 'I want to play hopscotch happily with my friends'). <br><br> In this case you ask '... and when (remedy without the 'want', i.e. as though it has been achieved: 'they stop chasing you') then what happens?' |
| Step 4 | Ask '... and what needs to happen for that to happen?' |
| Step 5 | Ask '... and is there anything else that needs to happen?' |
| Step 6 | Ask '... and can that happen?' |

Children will often come to their own solutions in the space of a few questions. At times you may find you need to go through a few more rounds of questioning to arrive at a resolution that satisfies all involved. You can see how this works in action in the example below (you can find a more detailed explanation of this process in Chapter 6).

## Star Wars and light sabers

| Jimmy: | She punched me in the face and it hurt and I don't like it. |
|---|---|
| Misha: | Well, it was an accident and, anyway, he kicked my leg and I told him to stop and he kept kicking and it hurt my leg. |

Me: And she punched you in the face and it hurt, and you don't like it. And when she punched and it hurt, and you don't like it, what would you like to have happen?

Jimmy: I want her to stop punching me.

Me (*to Jimmy*): And … you want her to stop punching you.

Me (*to Misha*): And it was an accident and he kicked your leg and you told him to stop and he kept kicking and it hurt your leg. And when accident and he kept kicking and it hurt your leg, what would you like to have happen?

Misha: THE TEACHER TELLS US OFF!

Me: And the teacher tells you off. And when the teacher tells you off, what would you like to have happen?

Misha: I want us to play nicely.

Me (*to Jimmy*): And … you want her to stop punching you. And when stop punching you, then what happens?

Jimmy: We can still play Star Wars but we don't get punched and stuff.

Me: And you can still play Star Wars but you don't get punched and stuff. And when you play Star Wars and you don't get punched and stuff, then what happens?

Jimmy: Well, we can play Star Wars and it's fun.

Me (*to Jimmy*): And … you can play Star Wars and it's fun.

Me (*to Misha*): And … you want 'us' (*looking at both of them*) to play nicely. And … what needs to happen for play Star Wars … fun … play nicely?

Misha: We can pretend to fight and not really hit and that's playing nicely.

Jimmy: Yeah, we can pretend to use light sabers and go whaaa, whaaa, whaaa, so we can do pretend attack with light sabers and get them like that (*demonstrating pretend capturing*), then we won't get hurt.

Me: And playing nicely … and pretend … and light sabers … And can that happen?

Both children (*talking at the same time*): Yes, we can have light sabers and just pretend, whaaa, whaaa …

At this point I gestured (*a palms-up shrug gesture*) and they both went off to play nicely, capturing each other and using imaginary light sabers – and I had missed a wonderful opportunity to tell them off!

When children experience this model for clean conflict resolution, they soon begin to internalise the process and use it for themselves. It also offers them an excellent model for listening which they are able to adopt for more effective interaction in the classroom.

## Working according to agreed principles

All schools have a behaviour policy and it's important for any such policy to be adhered to consistently throughout the school. Policies that are focused at the level of behaviour tend to have a list of specific rules (e.g. 'walk in the classroom', 'work quietly') and specific rewards for compliance. Carefully constructed, clearly communicated and consistently adhered to they successfully bring about pupils' conformity with the rules.

When behaviouristic policies like this are expressed less clearly, for instance, mixing behaviour-based descriptions with values-based descriptions (e.g. 'value possessions', 'no inappropriate language', 'give homework in on time', 'do not run') or when principles are confused with rules, they become difficult or impossible to stick to consistently and the results are haphazard.

When behaviour policies are based on agreed principles (values that support learning) which are generated by all learners, and when learners have real ownership of those policies, they become motivated and engaged within the learning culture they have created. Pupils who are self-motivated and engaged naturally work towards success – for themselves and for the learning group. Clean questions help to ensure that the learning needs and values which are adopted into policies are indeed the learners' own needs and values. A clean approach encourages learner autonomy, competence and a connection to those shared values – it promotes a strong learning culture.

# Chapter 10
# Mathematician Magicians

Mathematics is the art of explanation.

Paul Lockhart and Keith Devlin, *A Mathematician's Lament* (2009)

A clean approach can facilitate the development of mathematical thinking in a number of ways. If children are to fully engage with mathematics, it's important for them to develop a level of resilience and trust. Maths is a subject that on the one hand is commonly viewed as free from affect (i.e. it's rational, objective and based on cool, clear thinking rather than emotion) and on the other, people's approach to it is often steeped in emotion. Mathematicians may have a positive passion for their subject but many people are terrified at the thought of it.

I use a clean approach to facilitate children's mathematical thinking. This develops their competencies and encourages them to become more aware of the emotional processes they experience as they are working, which also helps them to gain in confidence. Approaching the subject from both these angles creates a virtuous circle where confidence supports competence and vice versa.

A clean culture reinforces the value of diversity, helping children to feel comfortable to share their ideas, respect differences in approach and be OK with failure – because they all know they have something worthwhile to contribute whether their answer is right or wrong. When they explore strategies and mathematical ideas as a team, it is as interesting to explore a team member's wrong answer and find out where they went wrong as it is to find correct answers – it's all mathematics.

When children work as mathematicians they will inevitably become stuck at some point. When stuck they can experience frustration, fear and all kinds of disabling reactions, or they can tap into a level of resilience to see them through the challenge. If they model their reactions and become more aware of their emotional processes (their feelings) they can become less caught up in them. They can learn to notice their patterns of reaction and work through them rather than avoid feeling them. This will give them the resilience they need to persevere with challenging problems through to completion rather than give up. It also allows them to cope with any 'failure' they may experience along the way.

Many children (and adults) experience sensations which signal whether they have got the answer right or wrong. Some sensations say, 'Go back and check'; some sensations indicate, 'I get it!' They may have an awareness sensation which indicates a 'pattern is emerging' or they may get a 'feel' of the structure of a problem. These sensations, emotional feelings, their maths process and their answers all constitute feedback in the process of learning.

Take some time to reflect and become more aware of the sensations you experience (sensory feedback) during your own learning.

- How do you know when you are on the right track?

- How do you know when you get something (understand it)?

- How do you know when your answer is right?

Many children equate success in mathematics with 'getting answers right'. But when engaging at their learning edge it's not about getting everything right first time. It's about them stepping into unknown territory (which is risky) and it's about them trusting that they will emerge intact, no matter what. When children have such faith in themselves and recognise that their feelings are precisely that (sensations in their bodies) they can delight in challenge, rather than recoil from it, and become courageous learners.

It's easy to underestimate how much courage some children need to muster in order to move beyond their fear. A clean approach helps them develop the courage to persevere when they are stuck, unsure or don't know. It also helps children to model resourceful responses to being stuck, unsure or not knowing (you can find an example of this in Chapter 17). In this way, children can reflect on their own responses and those of others in the same way as they reflect on other aspects of their learning.

Focusing on the mathematics itself, clean questioning provides a structure to model mental strategies systematically. Children soon adopt the DDQs to interrogate their own and others' thinking. This helps them to be more flexible in their approach and they are able to try out other children's methods. They learn that there can be a variety of ways to address a mathematical problem, that people may choose different routes to a solution and that we can learn from each other through cooperative engagement. Lockhart and Devlin (2009: 31) assert that 'Math is not about following directions, it's about making new directions.'

Here's how I've used the clean questions to explore mathematical thinking in class. In the lesson excerpt that follows, individual children volunteer to demonstrate how they solve 26 + 5, explaining their strategies while the other children check out (model) the thinking and compare it with their own ways of working.

Joy comes up to the board and draws a ladder. She labels the first rung 26 and then describes her strategy, demonstrating how she steps up the ladder as she counts on in 1's: 26 + 1 + 1 + 1 + 1 + 1 = 31. Graham's number line is horizontal. He jumps along a mental number line in 2's, then he adds 1: 26 + 2 = 28 + 2 = 30 + 1 = 31. Tony also draws a horizontal number line, starts at 26, counts on 4, then adds 1: 26 + 4 = 30 + 1 = 31. He explains how he uses a recall of number bonds, '6 + 4 = 10, so we have 20 + 10 = 30 + 1 = 31.'

I support the volunteers to relate their strategies by asking clean questions ('And then what happens?', 'And what happens next?', 'And what happens just before (...)?', 'And whereabouts is (...)?'). As each volunteer completes their demonstration I thank them for their contribution and ask the class, 'And who does the same as ...? And who does something different?'

I invite them to 'Do it now, 26 + 5, and notice ... notice what happens.' Children then share their strategy with a talk-partner.

> Who does it *exactly* the same as their partner?
>
> Wow nobody!
>
> Hmm ... interesting ... OK, so now we're going to do a little bit of thinking about our thinking.
>
> Tell me something *you* notice that you do *differently* from your partner – *or* that your partner does differently from you ... What are the differences?
>
> How do you know that you don't do it exactly the same as your partner?
>
> How do you know?

We share, briefly, a few examples:

> Jodie: Mine is curved.
>
> Me: Oh, yours is curved ... and whereabouts curved?

Jodie: It's there and it's curved (*across the side of her head, curving over her eyebrow*).

Me: So Jodie's is there ... and it's curved.

Annusha: I imagine a ruler.

Me: Oh ... and you imagine a ruler ... and is there anything else about a ruler?

Annusha: I see a ruler and I see a hand going along the ruler (*she demonstrates*).

Me: Oh look ... Annusha imagines a ruler and a hand goes along like this ...

... notice what it's like ...

... and what happens for you?

Jeanne: I count on.

Me: ... and when counting on like that ... what kind of counting on?

Jeanne: I'm just thinking 1, 2, 3 or something.

Me: Ahh ... and when you are just thinking 1, 2, 3 like that ... how do you know?

Jeanne: Because I can feel it.

Me: ... and you can feel it ... and whereabouts *feel it*?

Jeanne: There (*she points to her head*).

Me: ... and *there* (*pointing to her head*) ... and whereabouts *there*?

Jeanne: There (*pointing, more precisely, to the side of her head*).

Me: Oh, *there* ... and when you feel it *there* ... what kind of feeling is that?

(*Jeanne describes the feeling*)

The final four questions asked of Jeanne focus her attention on her thinking. As she becomes more aware of her thinking, where it happens for her and what it's like, she builds her capacity to notice and focus on her mental strategies. In time she will be able to describe these strategies to others, but before she can do that she needs to have an awareness of them. Clean questions enable such metacognitive reflection.

The children return to comparing strategies with their talk-partners for two minutes before they begin to work some more examples. I give them a challenge to experiment with each other's strategies to find solutions. The concluding part of the lesson consists of sharing some of the examples. We acknowledge the range of differences and that it's OK to use your own strategy. We explore which of the strategies are most efficient (quick and easy) and which are not useful for the particular problem.

Here is how one child works mentally with 17 + 12:

Dan:     I get the 17 and the 12 yeah.

Me:      ... and you get the 17 and the 12 ...

         ... and when you *get* the 17 and the 12, whereabouts do you get them?

Dan:     I get them there (*in a space about 15 cm in front of his forehead, the 17 is to his left and the 12 is to his right about 30 cm apart*).

Me:      ... and you get them there. Hmm ... and then what happens?

Dan:     Well, I put the 2 over there for a bit (*he grabs the 2 from the 12 and places it down to the right at about waist height, about 45 cm in front of his body*) so I can remember I've got it – because that was 12 and now it's 10. Then I put the 10 with the 17 and that's easy, it's 27.

Me:      Ahh, you put the 10 with the 17 and that's easy ...

         ... and when it's easy like that ... what kind of easy?

| Dan: | Well, you just do 10 add 10 is 20 and then you put the 7 back on so it's 27. |
|------|------|
| Me: | Oh ... it's that kind of easy ... you just do the 10 add 10 is 20 ... |
| | ... and then you put the 7 back on ... |
| | ... and then what happens? |
| Dan: | Well, you get the 2 and then it's 29 (*he grabs the 2 from where he'd left it down by his waist and places it up in front of his fore-head with the 27*). |

Dan has a clear awareness of his strategy. You can see how the questions encourage him to consider each step of the strategy and to notice not just what he does but how he does it and where. His mental manipulations are brought to life so clearly that they are almost physically tangible.

We can all see how he does it – literally *see* it, as well as understand it. We watch his gesticulations as he grabs hold of an imaginary 2 and places it in a specific space beside his waist, and later we watch him retrieve it from the exact spot in which he had left it and place it back in front of his forehead.

When children observe each other's thinking set out clearly before them like this they are able to try it on for size and, if it fits the bill, adopt it for themselves. It's easier for children to demonstrate their thinking 'live' than it is to explain it purely verbally. It's more concrete. It's also easier for the other children to take on a new strategy when they see it played out like this than to follow purely verbal explanations of it. Clean modelling helps children to communicate more than they can say.

As the children become familiar with multiple ways of working they are able to evaluate the strategies they have modelled, to identify those that are most suited to the purpose of the current mathematical problem and to rank them according to speed and ease of use. Sometimes there is a clear consensus in class as to the most appropriate and efficient method. At other times opinions are split.

There are occasions when an individual child will appreciate the merits of another child's strategy but will choose to stick with their own current method because they don't yet have the skills to perform the more efficient one. For instance, in a problem that requires the child to know how many 5p coins there are in 35p, the child may recognise that another child's multiplication strategy is quick and easy to use but will still choose to draw 5p coins and use fingers to count up in 1's (in groups of five) until they reach 35. They appreciate that multiplication is the more efficient method but they don't know their 5 times table yet, so the counting method is their most efficient way for the time being.

More often than not, when children make observations and come to their own conclusions like this, a desire is ignited – a motivation to take the next steps in their learning – and learning becomes compelling. In the example described here, the child came to appreciate the benefits of learning the times tables and set out to do just that.

Lockhart and Devlin (2009: 15) remind us:

> If you deny students the opportunity to engage in this activity – to pose their own problems, make their own conjectures and discoveries, to be wrong, to be creatively frustrated, to have an inspiration, and to cobble together their own explanations and proofs – you deny them mathematics itself.

# Chapter 11
# Speaking and Listening

Speaking and listening skills are a foundation for literacy and play a central role in effective communication. In Chapter 7 I outlined how I introduce young children to clean questions and explained how show and tell sessions offer a context in which to practise them. In this chapter I reflect on how clean questions can enhance students' speaking and listening skills, using an example of a workshop conducted with older children.

## Listening for Life

I was invited to deliver a workshop for Year 7 students as part of a PSHE day in a Cambridgeshire secondary school. My brief was to present a session on listening called 'Listening for Life'. I ran the same 50-minute session five times during the day for five different classes. I had been informed that there would be no time for subsequent follow-up so the session was designed to stand alone.

## Group rules

I started by asking the students what rules they would like to make for the session. The students were happy for me to tinkle a tiny bell after each activity to signal a quick stop and to maintain pace, given the limited time available. The children suggested rules such as, listen when someone is speaking, listen to one another, don't talk over people and put your hand up to talk. This was not surprising given the title of the session – children often try to please their teacher by second guessing what they think the teacher wants or is expecting to hear.

I'm reminded of a story I heard about a vicar who came into school to conduct an assembly ...

The vicar arrived on a sunny day in autumn and began his assembly by commenting on the beautiful colours of the autumnal leaves on the oak tree outside.

He went on to talk about the autumn season, the acorns and a small fluffy tailed creature that lives in the trees in the school grounds. He asked, 'Does anyone know what that creature might be?' A child replied, 'Yes, it's Jesus.' The vicar asked again and was asked, 'Is it God?' He was perplexed. He tried in vain to coax an appropriate answer from the children but they were all intent on giving him an answer they thought he would want to hear, based on their understanding of the context they were in. After all, he was a vicar and this was a school assembly – the answer must be 'Jesus', mustn't it? Interestingly, the children were just as perplexed when he revealed the creature was a squirrel!

A clean approach can help to minimise the common tendency to anticipate answers like this. The students in the listening workshop were already second guessing so my attention was on facilitating, using a clean approach to direct the focus of their attention to their own thoughts and contributions, rather than on trying to guess mine.

## Listening and life

I asked, 'What has listening got to do with life?' After a short time reflecting with a partner the students offered a range of answers which were summarised and grouped into three categories: you learn more, you get a better job and you make better friendships. Their ideas were noted and displayed on a board, then we moved on to the first activity.

## See an elephant[1]

This activity was for groups of three or four students. They were all asked to 'see an elephant' (to imagine one in their mind's eye) and then to take turns describing it to the others in their group, who then asked DDQs to elicit more detail about what the elephant was like. I suggested they use some of the following questions, choosing one that fitted well with what the 'elephant imaginer' had said:

• What kind of (...)?

---

1   This activity was devised by Caitlin Walker.

- Is there anything else about (...)?

- Whereabouts is (...)?

- Does (...) have a size or a shape?

Bear in mind that these students hadn't been introduced to the DDQs prior to the event. (For this exercise they didn't need an explanation about the questions. I wrote them on the flip chart and they just used them.)

## Different elephants

Having questioned each other in their group about their elephants, the class came together to share. They took turns to describe the elephant they had imagined in their mind's eye. Each elephant was different from the next. There were grey elephants, pink elephants, rainbow coloured elephants, realistic elephants, cartoon-like elephants, Indian elephants, African elephants, flying elephants, walking elephants, charging elephants, floating elephants, big elephants and small elephants. Some standing, some lying, some were whole elephants and some were features of an elephant (e.g. trunk or head).

Students in each session responded with surprise that not a single person in the class had imagined the same elephant. There were around 30 different interpretations of the word 'elephant' in every class. For a few students, the results were in line with their expectations but for most it was a revelation. All students were surprised at the extent of the differences between the elephants, and readily appreciated the significance of the results in relation to communication.

They then went on to consider questions that had arisen as a result of the experience:

- If individuals interpret words in such idiosyncratic ways (like we've just seen with the word 'elephant'), what does it mean for communication generally?

- If we have completely different interpretations of every word we use, how on earth do we manage to understand each other at all?

This short activity gave the students a direct experience of something they had probably only noticed the effects of before. These effects appear in the form of miscommunication and misunderstandings in their everyday lives.

As students become aware of the idiosyncratic nature of interpretations, they become less judgemental when communication goes awry and more sensitive to the challenges of clear communication. As they continue to reflect on the questions raised, they will appreciate more than most that good listening and questioning are vital for effective communication. This perspective is especially pertinent for teenagers.

## Three listening activities

Students worked in pairs for three rounds of listening. In each round, one student was nominated 'speaker' and the other 'listener', and when the activity was complete they were instructed to swap roles and repeat it. What changed in each round was the way the students were required to listen.

- In the first activity, the listener was instructed to sit still like a statue.

- In the second, the listener was instructed to fidget (or do anything they liked) as long as they could hear and recall what was said.

- In the third, the listener was instructed to 'do good listening'. They drew on their own current understandings of what good listening might entail (including any insights they had gained from the workshop so far). In addition, the speaker was instructed to coach the listener to do more of 'what works for them' by giving feedback in the moment so the listeners could become better listeners. For example:

  > Marking moments when they were feeling heard: 'Now ... now ... now.'

  > Marking actions: 'When you nod like that ...', 'When you raise your eyebrows ...'

  > Providing feedback about the behaviour along with information about their interpretation of that behaviour: 'When you look towards me like that, I get the sense that you are paying attention to me.'

Afterwards, I asked the speakers to record how they felt in each round. The results are shown in the table below.

| Listener sitting still | Listener fidgeting | Good listening |
|---|---|---|
| Awkward. | I felt annoyed. | I felt happy. |
| Boring. | I wanted to hit him. | Jolly. |
| I felt strange when there was no feedback from the listener. | Frustrated. | Appreciated. |
| | Aggravated. | Respected. |
| I felt exposed with no feedback. | Angry. | Thankful. |
| | Bored. | |
| I thought they might think I was stupid and they weren't doing anything to contradict that. | It made me laugh. | |

## What kind of listening is good listening?

After the activities were finished, I asked: 'What kind of listening is good listening?' The students in each class developed a definition for good listening based on their own experiences in the activity and in life. Although different in detail, there was clear consensus across the classes:

- Look at the person.

- Make appropriate faces.

- Stay reasonably still but not stiff.

- Smile.

- Nod.

- Make appropriate sounds.

I asked, 'Is good listening the same for everyone?' The students found exceptions to the examples – eye contact for instance: some people don't like to be looked at when they are being listened to because it makes them feel uncomfortable. The students realised that they need to monitor the speaker's responses in order to fine-tune their listening behaviour to suit the individual.

I asked, 'How much energy does it take to do "good listening"?' The students agreed that it doesn't take much energy to do good listening; it takes about the same as doing 'bad listening' (their description). I reminded them that they have the power to choose.

## Listening to yourself

I asked, 'Have you ever taken a moment to listen to yourself?' Some had, some hadn't. I invited them to take a moment to listen right now … this moment … I invited them to tune in to themselves like this as often as they wished and to discover how helpful, or not, their own inner voice was (e.g. What do you say to yourself when you make a mistake? For instance, do you say, 'You idiot!'? What would be a supportive thing to say? What would you like to say to yourself instead? What might be the result of talking to yourself differently?).

## And knowing all of that … what difference does it make?

Reflecting on the session as a whole, I asked:

> … and knowing all of that … what difference does it make?

> … and what would you like to have happen next … as you walk out of the door … for the rest of the day … tomorrow … in a week … and the months that follow?

> … and what needs to happen … for that to happen?

The students shared their responses with a partner. Their responses served as mini action plans for them to take away and refer to in the days and weeks that followed.

## After the session

Feedback from the teachers was positive. One teacher who participated in the process said, 'I'm blown away!' He described it as, 'So simple yet profound.' The colleague who had invited me (and who'd said there would be no time for follow-up) now said that she was definitely going to follow it up. The head teacher said, 'There are a fair few adults who could benefit from learning this!'

A few weeks later the colleague wrote to say: 'The PSHE day had some very positive responses especially from staff who attended the sessions and also the students themselves. Some staff said your session was the best session they experienced that day.' She could see great potential in 'integrating a Clean Language approach into the curriculum methodology with the aim of achieving the learning objectives effectively, efficiently and with elegance'.

## Six months later

My colleague sent an update regarding her follow-up:

> I have been using clean questions at the start of lessons to introduce the subject and this makes for a good start. I also use them for discussion. There is *no doubt* the students are made to think much more. I have also incorporated clean questions into the student's design technology work booklets by changing the phrasing of the existing questions into a clean format. The effect has been more detailed answers and their answers are more carefully thought through.

## Four years later

The colleague was still using clean questions to good effect with her design and technology students:

> I use clean questions in the project booklets. I also use it in discussion. You get more of a response. When they give me an answer I say, 'What kind of ...?', and there's more of a dialogue. When I ask, 'And is there anything else?', the children come up with more and more things.
>
> It changed the dynamics of the teacher–pupil relationship and it 'switched them on' into thinking further. It stopped being a 'teacher led' thing and became more of a dialogue. I used it on a one-to-one basis as well and the children would think more about what they were going to do. It engaged their brains in a non-pressurised way.

It was rewarding to see how this 50 minute one-off session had acted as a catalyst for ongoing development in teaching and learning.

# Chapter 12
# Reading

Reading happens in many different contexts in classrooms and a clean approach can facilitate progress in various ways. You can use clean questions in everyday reading work, blending them with your usual teaching approach; you can use Symbolic Modelling to develop 'reading at my best' states and effective reading strategies; and you can adopt a clean coaching approach to support pupil progress towards their reading targets.

I began to use clean questions in reading activities by just using them conversationally whenever I worked with individuals in one-to-one reading sessions. You can dovetail clean questions with your current teaching practices, whether you are working on reading with an individual, a group or your whole class. When children work individually or in pairs on a text, they can use their DDQ magnifying glasses as prompts for stimulating their own reflections or for questioning their partner, using clean questions alongside any other questions that arise.

Symbolic Modelling can be used with a child to enable them to identify and develop their best reading state or for them to evolve an effective reading behaviour or strategy. You can use it to model motivation for reading, reading confidence or any other attitude that supports reading (e.g. When I'm reading at my best *I'm* like what? When I'm reading at my best *it's* like what? When I'm skimming/scanning/inferring (insert any reading strategy in here) at my best *it's* like what?). Alternatively, a child who wants to raise their skill level can model another child who already has the skill they would like to embody. Children can model reading behaviours, attitudes and beliefs (see Chapter 5). It's also possible for the whole class to model an individual with a particular strength, so that everyone can 'try it on for size'.

As children are working towards their 'next step' targets, you can use Clean Language in a coaching framework to promote progress and goal achievement. You will recall the child (in Chapter 7) who wanted her daddy to stop patting her on the head and to start giving her a kiss on the head when she correctly deciphered an unknown word. The questions helped her to identify what she wanted to have happen and to make a plan of action in order to achieve her outcome.

When children are facilitated to address their own progress and make their own next step outcomes, along with plans to achieve them, you will find these plans fit them like a glove. When children are facilitated cleanly like this, they can address needs that you would never have known were there and the outcomes they create will be bespoke. What's more, children become more capable of recognising their learning needs and more effective in asserting them.

The knock-on effects in terms of raised self-confidence and self-esteem aren't just in relation to reading; these gains are transferable across the curriculum and across all aspects of their lives.

> Five-year-old Mark wanted to be good at reading. And anything else about that? He wanted to be able to read a stage 5 book independently. And what needed to happen for that to happen? He needed to be good and work hard. And when he worked hard like that … what kind of hard? 'Well, helping my mummy with the washing up and tidying my toys away.'
>
> We modelled some good readers in class and he discovered that good readers *practise reading* rather than working hard at helping mummy. As a result, he changed his approach accordingly and made accelerated progress; I learned the value of a little clean questioning to uncover misunderstandings which may otherwise so easily remain hidden; and mum took on the washing-up because now he constantly had his nose in a book.

It can be easy to miss barriers to learning, as we are often seduced by our own assumptions and don't look beyond them. The experience described above serves as a reminder to take a clean approach and remain open to whatever emerges. It helps me to remember to remain vigilant and curious – to remain alert to what might be just outside of my awareness.

## Practice task

Ask yourself:

- What are *you* missing?

- What kinds of misunderstanding are happening in your classroom, right now?

# Chapter 13
# Narrative Writing

Without the basic skills of language and listening, children are not going to be able to develop their literacy skills ... The thing is to ask questions or give commentaries which will open language, not close it.

Sue Palmer and Ros Bayley, *Foundations of Literacy* (2013)

## Characterisation

Once the children have developed an informal familiarity with clean questions, characterisation is a great place for them to start to practise using them with their talk-partner more formally in lessons. For example, you can tell the story of the 'Three Billy Goats Gruff' and ask the children to draw a scene from the story including at least one of the characters. The children can then work with a talk-partner, asking each other clean questions about the characters in their picture. To start the process off, a child may point to something in their talk-partner's picture and ask, 'What's that?', or the child who drew the picture may begin by describing one of the charac-ters. Then they continue by using the DDQs and adopting the role of 'detail detective' to find out more.

Jenny: What's that?

Pat: That's the troll.

Jenny: And is there anything else about that troll?

Pat: He has black hair.

Jenny: Black hair ... and what kind of hair is that black hair?

Pat: It's long, curly, black hair.

In response to the DDQs from their talk-partner, most children will give additional information beyond that which is evident in the picture. As the questioning reveals further detail, the children update their picture by drawing in the new information. In the example above, for instance, the troll's hair was altered to look long and curly, when it had previously been indistinct but certainly straight and short.

The DDQs can be used to elicit even more detail if you use them in combination with other approaches to explore characterisation with the children – for example:

- **Role-play:** where children act out scenes from the story using the questions to inform the director's decisions – setting up the scene and exploring characters' attributes (e.g. appearance, behaviour, motivations).

- **Hot-seating:** where a child takes on the role of a character and fields questions from the other children while remaining in character.

- **Building a comparison chart:** where aspects of one character (e.g. age, gender, appearance, style of dress, motivation, behaviour, speech) are compared and contrasted with those of other characters in the same story or with characters from other stories.

The children soon notice that the DDQs help to extract additional information. With experience, they come to realise that the questions offer a framework for the questioner to focus attention on one aspect at a time and this framework helps them to sense when to shift the focus to another aspect. Using the DDQs like this also establishes a context for thinking and talking about questions and questioning.

# Plot

When starting to consider the plot of a story (either their own or a retelling of another author's tale), children often draw the events in a series of snapshots. They may construct a text-map or draw pictures for a storyboard before developing ideas at word or sentence level, which eventually leads on to the creation of a complete story. They may act out a story that has been read to them and practise retelling it orally before committing anything to paper. Maybe they will attempt a first draft using scaffolding to aid planning or by enhancing a text-map or storyboard with symbols, drawings and key vocabulary. They may complete planning grids with ideas for the beginning, the middle and the end of the story. Whatever your approach, sprinkling DDQs into the mix will help the children attend to (and create) more detail in their written work.

When the children use DDQs at each stage of their planning, they can quickly and easily increase the quantity and the quality of the detail they bring to their work. It's quite simple to infuse your current approach with the DDQs to amplify the impact. For example, you can add DDQs to your own delivery during the lesson, get the children to ask each other DDQs in pairs as their work develops, or use DDQs to extend the thinking of individual children as you (or your teaching assistant) move around the room, supporting children as they work.

As a strategy it's simple, quick and purposeful, and it trains the children's attention on the work in hand rather than on conversation with the teacher, teaching assistant or talk-partner. It reveals information that might otherwise remain hidden and so facilitates creative flow.

# Timelines

Combining the use of DDQs and a timeline can be particularly effective because it allows a child to make changes and add additional detail to the plot (before an event, after an event, between events) prior to it being set in stone in the form of a storyboard or written text. A timeline is an excellent planning tool because it's simple and flexible. You can use a timeline in a practical way (by writing it down on paper) or as a mental process (by visualising it).

To make a story timeline, take a strip of paper (real or imaginary) and draw a line horizontally along it from beginning to end. Mark the beginning of the story at one end with a vertical line and label it in whatever way you choose. Choose something that will remind you what happens at the beginning of the story – perhaps an icon, a quick sketch, a word, phrase or sentence. Now you can mark another key part of the story in the same way. For instance, you may like to place the conclusion of the story at the other end of the paper or an event that occurs around the middle of the story in the middle of your timeline. Just plot the key details, wherever they need to be, along the line from beginning to end, labelling each point so that you will remember what it represents. This can be a convenient point to take a break.

Once you have mapped out the key points of the plot, the next step is to develop it. Choose one of the labelled points on the timeline and ask, 'What's happening?' When you have an answer you may want to ask a few DDQs to elicit a little more detail (e.g. '... and is there anything else about (...)?', '... and what kind of (...)?', '... and whereabouts is (...)?'). This isn't essential for every point along the line, of course.

You can also examine areas of the timeline to find out if events in the plot can be enhanced or added to by asking (inserting the name of an existing event into the brackets):

- What happens just before (...)?

- What happens just after (...)?

- What happens just after (...) and just before (...)?

- And what's between (...) and (...)?

(See Chapters 3 and 5 for how to formulate the questions.)

When you first start to use DDQs combined with a timeline, it's best for the children to work with a partner, taking turns to ask each other the questions. This means one child can focus on the questioning strategy while the other focuses on answering the questions and discovering more about their story. As they become familiar with the process, the children will be able to use it independently as an internal mental strategy.

You may choose to develop only one part of the story – for instance, the beginning, the middle, a particular event or the ending. When children first begin story writing, their endings often peter out so you may want to spend some time developing the ending right from the start. When they use a timeline, children can work from the ending back to the beginning, from the beginning to the end or from any point in between – whatever suits the individual, the task and the context.

It's surprising how much more detail children can generate about a story when they use DDQs – they usually know much more than they (or we) realise. The questions are a great way of teasing out a child's creativity and can help latent ideas to emerge. And because a timeline is so simple (i.e. it doesn't require elaborate pictures or pre-designated spaces like a storyboard), it's an extremely flexible tool – it can be altered and adjusted as new information emerges. It's perfectly possible to splice (cut and paste) the timeline to make room for additional information or to change the order of events. It's so much quicker and easier to do this with a timeline than with a beautifully illustrated storyboard or a handwritten first draft.

Children can insert a new idea and then add in knock-on effects that might arise later in the story. As they add details to an ending, for example, they may realise that certain key information will need to be inserted at the beginning. A facet of a particular character might need to be alluded to in the introduction, for instance, or a completely new character might be required to make the story hang together effectively. In this way children learn to weave story elements together systematically, being flexible and responsive to emerging ideas, without lengthy and demotivating drafting and redrafting.

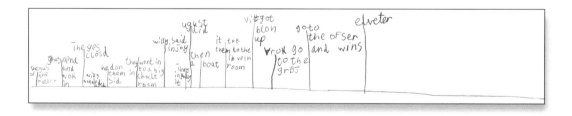

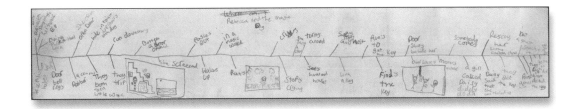

Most experts on children's literacy promote oral storytelling as a basis for children's writing development. When children use a timeline to guide their oral storytelling their contributions can be augmented using the DDQs in a conversational way. Older children can use these methods to investigate story structures and patterns or as a planning tool for their own story writing – and again the DDQs can be used to enrich their work as described above. In time, they can go without a paper timeline as they internalise the process and use it to develop their ideas mentally.

## Story direction cards

Story direction cards are a content-free way of stimulating ideas for a story (see Appendix C). They make use of the idea of chunking.[1] I developed the story direction cards to enable children to access a resourceful state and generate imaginative ideas to support their writing in a classroom environment. Having

---

1   I first experienced how chunking can support storytelling during a workshop on storytelling presented by Pamela Gowler-Wright. Pamela developed the idea from improvisation techniques to enhance teaching and creative thinking.

learned to play with them in a class situation, the children are soon able to play with independence in small groups or on their own. They can be used along with a timeline and DDQs to expand detail or they can be used in a stand-alone fashion. Children can make their own set of cards to keep as a personal resource for inspiring content creation for their writing (as in the examples below). And just like the timeline, once they get to grips with this practical resource, they will soon begin to hold the idea as a mental strategy to inspire their thinking. Children have found the strategy very useful for generating ideas for writing in test conditions.

Children decided that an 'up arrow' on the card could signify anything you might associate with an upward transition, the 'sideways arrow' could signify anything you might associate with adjacency and the 'down arrow' could signify anything you might associate with a downward transition.

The following table includes examples of some of the words and ideas the children in one class categorised according to the arrows.

| Up arrow | Down arrow | Sideways arrow |
|---|---|---|
| Zooming out | Zooming in | Right or left |
| Higher | Worse | Next to |
| Rising to life | Falling | Beside |
| Jumping | Plunging | Around |
| Flying | Going lower | Directions |
| *More* dramatic or nervous | Underground | Alone |
| • Crazy | Shrinking/shrunk | Together |
| • Serious | Getting colder | Family |
| • Funny | *Less* dramatic – calmer | Brother(s) |
| • Exciting | • Sleepier | Sister(s) |
| • Scary | • Quieter | Daughter(s) |
| • Sad | • Slower | Son(s) |
| • Happy | • Gentler | Mother(s) |

| *More* things | *Fewer* things | Father(s) |
|---|---|---|
| • Bigger | • Younger | Friend(s) |
| • Faster | • Smaller | Walking |
| • Harder | Gruesome | Swimming |
| • Louder | Sad | More detail |
| • Wider | Negative emotions | |
| • Longer | Slow | |
| • Better | | |
| • Getting warmer | | |
| • Hot/hotter | | |
| • Older | | |
| More positive emotions | | |

I encourage children to familiarise themselves with the cards and to explore their interpretation of the arrow directions by playing games with them. You can use the cards to play a game with the whole class, with a small group or solo:

- Shuffle the cards and place them in a pile within reach of all players. A volunteer flips the first card over and when it lands, whoever it points to starts the game. (If you are playing alone, skip this first step.)

- The first player begins the story with an opening (speaking aloud to the group). Any opening will do (e.g. 'Once upon a time there was a king …').

- The next player takes a card from the top of the pile, looks at the arrow they have been dealt and responds by creating the next part of the story (matching what they say to the direction of the arrow on their card). For instance, if they are dealt an 'up arrow' they might say, 'The king ruled over a massive kingdom', or 'The king was as tall as a house', or 'The king wore a crown of the most precious metal that ever there was, encrusted with the finest jewels in the kingdom' – anything that you might associate with up (see the table above for some ideas or invent your own).

- The next player then picks a card and adds to the story according to the arrow on it. Continue working around the group, adding to the story in accordance with the arrows on the cards as you go, and enjoy the story as it emerges.

It can be fun to record the story so the children can listen to it again later. Alternatively, if someone scribes as the game is being played, you can read the complete story to the children once you have finished playing.

The first time a group of children play the game it may be slow going, as they will need time to become familiar with the process and procedure. After a couple of rounds, though, it will liven up and then I've always found it to be a laugh a minute. Some of the stories that emerge can be so silly, which is OK because the aim at this stage is to break the ice. In time, the children will internalise the strategy and will be able to play without resorting to the cards. When writing, children often like to have the cards in front of them on the table as a reminder to consider the direction in which their story might go. Eventually they won't need the cards when they are writing either, as they will use the idea in their mind's eye as a tool to stimulate their ideas about plot.

# Setting

When you are working with story settings, whether the children are looking at a setting in a published text or working on developing an original setting in their own writing, they can use DDQs in much the same way as was described in the section above on characterisation. Starting from a picture, a visualisation or a written description, the children ask their talk-partner DDQs to elicit more than the surface information already known. Observe how the description is developed in the before and after examples below.

> It was a pirate ship. It was brown and it was made of wood with big sails.

> It is a light brown, wooden pirate ship (the size of five elephants). It has a big mast with four black, white and red flags, with a tiny one (a fifth one) at the top of the mast. The steering wheel is gold. At the back of the ship there is a bird's nest, with a pirate from the crew standing and looking out to sea. The front of the ship has a mermaid on it. Her tail is blue, her back is arched and she is looking up to the stormy sky. It is a really hot day. There is thunder and lightning and the boat is rocking side to side in the

bumpy sea. As rain is shooting down from the rainclouds the sun comes out and a pretty, colourful rainbow appears in the sky next to the pirate ship.

Children can also update their drawings as they become aware of any new information. This serves as a form of note-taking to support their subsequent writing. Again, you can see before and after examples below.

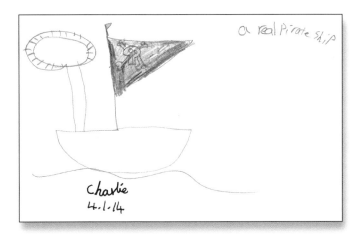

The location questions – '... and where is (...)?' and '... and whereabouts is (...)?' – are particularly relevant when developing a setting, along with the other developing questions – '... and is there anything else about (...)?' and '... and what kind of (...) is (...)?'

# Chapter 14
# Poetry

Poetry is an area of the curriculum where a clean approach and the use of DDQs can facilitate the development of the craft without stifling the art. A clean approach allows a teacher, or a child working with a talk-partner, to draw out understandings and insights without exerting their influence over the content of the work. In the example below, you can see how the children explore 'what makes a poem' and then create the success criteria for their own poem.

In this excerpt from a lesson, the children were discussing success criteria for the poetry work they were about to begin.

Chloe: Don't poems have to rhyme?

Me: Don't poems have to rhyme?

Trevor: Mine does.

Connell: Not always.

Marie: It doesn't have to as long as it's a good piece of work.

Me: And yours does ... and not always ... and a good piece of work ... and when we're writing poetry, is there anything else about 'a good piece of work'?

Trevor: It *can* rhyme and it might not rhyme.

Connell: It will have capital letters and full stops in the right places.

Me: And it can rhyme ... and it might not rhyme ... and it will have capital letters and full stops in the right places ... a good piece of work. And when 'a good piece of work', what kind of work is 'a good piece of work' ... when we're writing poetry?

Trevor: You have to make it so that whoever's reading it wants to read on and on and on, until the end.

Me: Hmmm ... yes ... and some poems do that, don't they? You want to read on and on until the end. And some poems that I've read have been as short as seven words and so there *is* no on and on and on!

... and if 'whoever' wants to read on and on and on, what kind of poem is a poem like that?

Pat: A poem with good words, like opening words and nouns and things ... words like that ... I'm not sure.

Me: ... and what kind of words in a poem would make you want to read on and on and on?

Trevor: The one I'm writing in my book makes me feel warm inside.

Marie: The one I'm doing makes me feel happy inside.

Pat: No matter what age it's done by, as long as it connects with the subject that the poem is about ... so ... as long as ... if it's about hopes and dreams, it needs to connect to hopes and dreams ... if it's about birds, it needs to connect to birds ... like that.

I share an example of a poem I like.

Me: I like the poem because it makes me feel ... it's a feeling of sadness. It's a safe sadness though – because I know it's not actually happening to me.

Tony: I like the tongue twister 'Peter Piper Picked a Peck of Pickled Pepper' because it makes me feel all weird and my tongue feels all tied up.

We all have a go at the tongue twister and feel it for ourselves. Some children attempt the tongue twister 'Red Lorry, Yellow Lorry, Red Lorry, Yellow Lorry' ... and we fall about laughing.

Me: You like a poem because it makes you feel warm.

You like a poem because it makes you feel happy.

You like a poem to connect like that.

I like a poem because it makes me feel sadness.

You like a poem because it makes you feel all 'weird'.

... and feel warm, feel happy, to connect, feel sadness, feel all 'weird' ... is there a relationship?

... feel warm ... feel happy ... to connect ... feel sadness ... feel all 'weird'?

The children discuss this with their talk-partners:

Pat: Happy and sad are opposite feelings.

Trevor: Happy and weird are fun feelings.

The children continue to share their thinking while I circulate and listen to them:

Me: So ... with a poem, is it the *taste* of it that makes it good?

Marie: No!

Me: Is it the *sight* of it that makes it good?

Pat: Sometimes.

Me: Sometimes ... sometimes it *is* the look of it, isn't it? – what it looks like on the page – the shape of the poem on a page.

Trevor: It's the feeling ... is it the feeling?

Me: The feeling? Hmmm ... think of a poem you like. Is it the feeling that makes it good?

Most children indicate, with a thumbs-up that the feeling is a key criterion.

Me: So, it's the feeling ... for most people ... also the look of it ... and also sometimes it might rhyme. For our success criteria then ... when you have written a good poem you'll know because ...

The children volunteered the following criteria:

- It will give you a feeling.

- It may look good on the page.

- It may have a pattern or rhyme.

- There's thought in the words or the pattern.

- It connects.

- Capital letters and full stops are in the right place.

  Me: ... so if you want to know if you've done a good poem, you can check it against that. If you've got all (or most) of these, you've got a good poem. Who already knew this (*the children indicate with their thumbs as before – most children did not know it before this conversation*)? Hmmm, well done, you've worked it out for yourselves.

Towards the conclusion of this part of the lesson, you will have noticed that my own preconceptions begin to dominate (not ideal – that's life!), but ultimately the success criteria are the children's, and they are left with a clear idea of what they are aiming for in their poetry.

As the children move on to compose their poems, they share their thoughts and question each other to foster inspiration and focus their thinking on the structure of their work. Children and adults in class use the DDQs to draw out insights about the structure of their poetry. Children use them to develop their own content in much the same way as described in Chapter 13. I use DDQs with the whole class to examine both published poems and the children's own work to spot patterns in the structure, in much the same way as we explore pattern in maths (see Chapter 10).

Another effective use of the DDQs in poetry writing is to take a talented class poet and model their process for writing poetry. When the children learn how the exemplar works they can use these insights to improve their own performance. Through the experience of modelling they also come to realise that there are more ways than previously imagined to create poetry. The range of approaches they (and you) will discover through modelling peers are magnificently diverse, and they often speak to fellow budding poets in ways that formal instruction can't match.

# Chapter 15
# Handwriting and Success Criteria

Our handwriting is very personal, a part of our self-image and an expression of our personality, just as the way we dress and present ourselves is.

**National Handwriting Association**

Handwriting is a complex skill. It requires us to coordinate ideas, words and sensory information, through motor control, to form symbols (i.e. letters and words) on a page. In order to write conventionally you need to know how to form the letters correctly but repetition embeds the skill. When you practice, you go over and over the same writing patterns until they become second nature – they become neurologically hardwired.

When you are engaged in this kind of learning (at your best), as distinct from developing concepts, you may have a different sense of yourself as a learner, and the conditions necessary for success may be different too. With physical skill-building, it's usually helpful to still your mind, to become composed ... focused ... empty.

When children reflect on 'learning at my best' during handwriting practice, they can sense what they are like and what they need, and are able to design optimal learning conditions for themselves. Most request a quiet space. We often play soft music and work in silence, and there is a meditative stillness in the air as the writing happens.

When I first introduce Clean Language for exploring success criteria, I often choose a handwriting session as the vehicle because the structure of these sessions has a predictable routine. I know the children will be more able to focus on the questions and on thinking about the success criteria because they are already familiar with the shape of the lesson.

Once the children know the learning outcome for the handwriting, I ask them to suggest the success criteria:

Jenna:     We will see changes in the handwriting.

Me:      We will see changes in the handwriting ... and what kind of changes will we see?

Jenna:   The handwriting getting neater.

Me:      Getting neater ... and is there anything else about neater? Discuss with your talk-partner.

The children consider 'neater' with their talk-partner, then we begin to share ideas. Actually they are perplexed:

Jenna:   It's just neater!

Me:      Hmm, yes, it's just neater ... and when it's just neater like that ... what *kind* of neater?

Jenna:   It won't be too small and it won't be too big. It will be just the right size.

Me:      ... and ... it won't be too small and it won't be too big. It will be just the right size ... and just the right size ... and when it's just the right size ... is there anything else about 'right' ... when it's just the right size?

Jenna:   Right as in correct ... it's the correct size.

Me:      Ahh ... it's the correct size ... hmm.

         (*I write 'the correct size' on the board*)

Me:      ... and ... handwriting ... and ... neater ... and ... it's the correct size (*pointing to the words on the board*) ... and neater ... and is there anything else about neater? Talk to your talk-partner.

Dan:     It needs to be straight.

Me:      Ahh ... straight ... and what kind of straight?

Dan:     Straight up or leaning over but still straight (*he gestures with his hands to show the two kinds of straight*).

Me:      Ahh ... straight up or leaning over but still straight ...

         (*I glance towards the place where he's gesturing*)

         ... and give me a word for that ...

         (*Glancing towards the 'gesture space' again – using gestures and glances in place of the words 'straight up' and 'leaning over'*)

Dan:     Angle ... the correct angle.

And we continue on in this manner until the children have built a useful list of success criteria.

In this example, the children were puzzled at first but they soon became familiar with the way of working and enjoyed offering their suggestions. The questions encouraged them to be more specific about the criteria than they had ever been before and by the end of the lesson we had established five success criteria for neater handwriting.

It needs to have (or be):

1. The correct shape.

2. The correct size.

3. In the correct space.

4. The correct angle (not sloping unless it's supposed to be).

5. Smooth flowing lines.

As children have generated these criteria themselves, they understand their relevance and are able to remember them and apply them in practice. Their criteria are certainly more pertinent and detailed than any I had set for them previously.

If children are to meet lesson objectives effectively, it's important that generalised terms (e.g. neater, better, doing something well or confidently) are clarified. How can you work to achieve something if you don't know what it is? Clean questions can facilitate children to clarify learning objectives for themselves and develop deeper understanding and ownership of the success criteria.

The first time I directed children's attention to success criteria in this way, it took almost half an hour, so little writing was completed. But the time it took to get clear about the criteria was time well spent and subsequent attempts were much quicker. Of course, this doesn't just apply to handwriting – clean questions can be used to establish clear success criteria in any subject. And this is why taking the time to set it up as a 'learning routine' makes it so worthwhile.

At intervals throughout a session, children work together with a talk-partner to assess their work against the criteria and to inform their own next steps. They follow a code, which they developed as a class, using clean questions to guide their observations and give feedback to each other. They mark examples with the appropriate letter whenever a criterion has been met and they identify the best examples in the piece (letters or words that meet all, or most, criteria).

# Class code for peer assessment

The correct shape: (Sh)

The correct size: (Si)

The correct space: (Sp)

The correct angle: (A)

Smooth flowing lines: (Sfl)

In this way, the children are fully involved in assessment for learning and can monitor their own progress collaboratively and independently.

Children can also be supported to identify their individual learning needs through the use of clean questions. (Flip back to page 126 and take a look at the conversation about handwriting which occurred during a story-writing session.) When a child identifies their own next step targets like this, not only does it give them a high level of ownership of the learning and the developmental task, but it also cuts the conversation down to a fraction of the time it would usually take to explain what needs to happen – and in a way which will be understood and acted upon.

Teachers spend a lot of time and attention devising next steps which align with the learning needs of their pupils. A clean approach facilitates the children to tailor the learning to their own exact requirements, in the moment. When children become personally involved with their learning like this, not only do they monitor, evaluate and plan for their own progress but the personal engagement also fosters their sense of handwriting as a means of personal expression, as something so much more than a drill.

# Chapter 16
# Science

## Light-bulb thinking

In science, as part of a topic on sound and light, the infant children took a walk around the school looking for sources of light. The objective was for them to be able to discriminate between natural and man-made sources. We ran through the activity together as a group first so the children could form clear expectations. Once the children were happy that they knew what to do, we prepared to set off on the 'light hunt'. They worked in pairs and I chipped in whenever necessary.

The children mostly used the clean questions: 'And what kind of (...)?', 'And is there anything else about (...)?' and 'And whereabouts is (...)?' One child experimented with 'Whereabouts is that light?' On consideration the class decided that, although the question seemed redundant, given that the light source has just been spotted (and therefore its position is known), it may still be useful to ask it to make sure the child who has identified it pays attention to its location, because it will help them to remember this when they reflect on their observations later, back in the classroom.

At this point, another child offered an idea: 'We could ask, "And then what happens?"' The class worked through an example together and everyone realised that it made little sense because 'And then what happens?' is useful for stories but not so appropriate for observations when we're not observing change, where nothing is happening. They agreed that all they were doing was spotting if the light was there, not noticing whether it was doing anything, so nothing happens next.

It was apparent that the children were learning something new about questioning, about language and about observational criteria before we had even started the activity. Everyone could tell that the question didn't add up in this context. Some children could generalise this realisation – they could see that some questions don't make sense in some contexts, that context makes a difference. Some were beginning to be able to articulate what it is that makes the difference.

We continued on with the activity and I introduced a new question: 'And where could that light come from?' The children made their way around the school, noting their findings and decisions. The new question sparked off some interesting discussions ...

| | |
|---|---|
| Chloe: | On the ceiling, in the skylight. |
| Sam: | And where could that light come from? |
| Chloe: | The light is coming through the skylight, from the sun. |
| Sam: | And is there anything else about the sun? |
| Chloe: | It's not just light, it's also hot. |
| Chloe: | (*spotting another*) There's one (*pointing to a fluorescent light on the ceiling*)! |
| Sam: | And what kind of light is that? |
| Chloe: | Man-made. |
| Sam: | And whereabouts is that light? |
| Chloe: | On the ceiling. |
| Sam: | And where could that light come from? |
| Chloe: | From electricity. |
| Me: | You might be interested to know that those strip lights are actually filled with gas. Electricity comes in through the end and the gas glows – making light. |
| Chloe: | The sun's a big ball of gas and it makes light – and that's a tube of gas and that makes light. The sun is natural and that's man-made. |

Chloe was grappling with the notion of the gas in the fluorescent tube and the gas of the sun and her categorisations of one as being man-made and the other as being natural. Chloe spent a long time thinking about this and sharing her dissonance with her talk-partner and the class, which stimulated further discussion about the nature of man-made and natural.

At first the class thought natural and man-made were opposites but following their discussion they concluded that man-made is a subset of natural, because humans are natural and everything they make originates from natural sources – even synthetic materials come from natural elements. This is pretty cool thinking for 5, 6 and 7-year-olds.

Of course, the clean questions were not the sole cause of the children having these discussions, but a clean foundation provides teachers with the structure they need to trust that children can be more resourceful than they may realise – to hold a space in which children can think and to feel confident facilitating children to their learning edge. When children are facilitated in their learning like this, they are stimulated to think, to recognise their thoughts and to feel comfortable articulating them – and we all learn together.

# Thinking about thinking

At the end of this lesson one child began to ask questions about the questions themselves. 'What's the difference between "Whereabouts is that light?" and "Where could that light come from?"' I suggested he use the two questions and, when asking them, notice any differences between the answers he received. I asked him to let me know whether the answers to the different questions were the same or different.

After he had checked it out he returned and reported excitedly, 'They're very different! The first one is whereabouts, *the place*, the other is whereabouts *in time*!' This explanation made good sense in the context in which he was working. He continued to reflect on it as he asked questions in different contexts and updated and refined his thinking as he went.

This is metacognitive reflection in action. I've yet to find a way to bring this about through didactic teaching or formal planning, but clean facilitation skills have helped me to be highly responsive to children in the moment, working flexibly within a framework which effectively extends their thinking from any given point, through the use of clean questions.

# Thinking about forces

A colleague in the classroom next door was keen to use Clean Language in her practice, having seen a big difference in the way the children were engaging in thinking in my class. She decided she would ask some clean questions during a science lesson. She knew the questions and had already spent some time practising them (asking and answering them with a couple of interested colleagues), but when the lesson was in full flow she found that she couldn't quite gauge the timing for delivery of her questions. She kept thinking, 'Shall I ask it now? … Shall it be now?'

It's surprising how challenging it can be to slip the questions into an interactive, whole-class session for the first time, and by lunchtime she had still not asked one. The lesson straddled lunch, so it was only half completed, and during the break my colleague explained what had happened and asked if I could give her some clues about *when* to ask a clean question. I thought it would be difficult to explain how to time the questions as the whole thing is context-dependent.

As it happened, I had a free period after lunch and she invited me to join her in her classroom to help identify suitable moments as they occurred. We agreed that I would model the questioning process for her. The lesson was about forces and the children were talking about toy cars and how they move, so I enquired about 'move'. I asked, 'And what kind of "move" is that move?' and the children responded with a lot of information. 'And is there anything else about that move?' elicited even more information. My colleague saw how to slip the questions in naturally and began to join in.

Simply by asking the children these questions, they identified that the distance a car travels is determined by how hard it is pushed. They began to speak about hard pushes and soft pushes and soon they were asking each other the clean questions, naturally and easily. They simply assumed that these are the kind of questions one asks when doing science.

A few questions later, one child pointed out that they would have to push all the cars with the same hand at the same time in order for an experiment to be fair. They realised that a push is a force. My colleague remarked that the information emerging was notably different to the children's contributions before lunch. They were more engaged in reasoning, they were more detailed in their observations and the class as a whole was more animated.

She wrote, 'And is there anything else?' at the top of her whiteboard and left it there as a reminder for the children to practise asking the question whenever they engaged in talk-partner discussions in class.

# Chapter 17

# Design and Technology

## Getting past stuck

Design and technology (D&T) is about creating a better future. It's about solving the problems of today by designing solutions for tomorrow. By its very nature, D&T has modelling at its heart. Children deconstruct products and use what they discover to make similar or improved products. They explore processes and decide whether to use them or adapt them for their own design purposes. Having designed products, they draw up plans for making them and they make them. They then evaluate their products in preparation for another round in a continuous cycle of improvement: identify need, design, make, evaluate, improve. Everything you have read previously about modelling (see Chapter 5) applies to designing and making in D&T.

Even young children can get to grips with obstacles in D&T. For instance, in an infant classroom where children were making puppets independently, they knew that the objective was to design a puppet, gather materials and develop cutting and sticking skills. Parent helpers assisted, not by cutting the cloth, selecting the materials or deciding how to join components, but by supporting the children to do it for themselves. And if the children needed help they were coached rather than told what to do or how to do it. The children knew that the aim was to grapple with ideas and overcome the obstacles that they *would* meet during the course of the project. Everyone was prepared to meet with frustration at some stage of the project and part of the learning was to develop ways to deal with it.

It's customary when stuck to try to find ways of coming up with new ideas using rubrics such as the one set out in the table below:[1]

| Stuck! | Think: Why you are stuck (e.g. I don't understand, I don't know what to do about ... , I can't see how to ... , I can't see why ...)? |
| --- | --- |

---

1   This rubric has been adapted from Mason et al. (1985), p. 18.

| Aha! | Take time to think, and maybe work with peers, on suggestions and ideas (e.g. Try … , Maybe … , But why …?). |
|---|---|
| Check | Check measurements and compare against original plan.<br>Check any insights through sketches and/or mock-ups.<br>Check your resolution meets the original criteria. |
| Reflect | Think about your approach to the problem: What did you do that worked well?<br>Consider positively what you can learn from the experience (this can be of use for future problem-solving). |

Rubrics help to guide our thinking, encouraging a shift from unresourceful to resourceful. Unfortunately, when learners become stuck, unresourceful emotions (fear, shame, embarrassment, etc.) can become intimately attached to their thinking. In an effort to deal with these emotions, learners develop strategies to avoid thinking problems through or to avoid the subject itself (e.g. entertaining unhelpful thoughts about self-worth). Some people experience this as a little voice inside their head saying, 'I can't do it', 'I'm useless at this' or 'I never get it right'. People's experiences of such thoughts differ – many experience them as a voice in or around their head saying something derogatory.

## Practice task

The next time you get stuck, take a moment to listen and notice what you are saying to yourself.

- Do you always think, feel and do the same things when you are stuck, or do you do different kinds of 'stuck' in different contexts?

- Notice what happens the next time you are stuck.

- Notice the difference that your noticing makes.

When people stop to focus on such thoughts for the first time they are often surprised at how disparaging the messages can be. We are often far harsher in our judgements of ourselves than we would ever dream of being to others. Neuroscience confirms that although many people aren't consciously aware of their avoidance strategies, nevertheless their emotional responses imperceptibly influence their cognition (see Schlöglmann, n.d.).

## Stuck thoughts tend to generate stuck feelings and stuck behaviours

If you think of the times you have ever been stuck, you will no doubt notice that you also *felt* stuck. You will probably also recall certain specific behaviours that accompany the stuck thoughts and feelings – for example, some people sigh, slump, pace around or clench their fists. When I'm stuck I sometimes shout '@*#!' inside my head (OK, sometimes out loud – but for the record I share this example with the children with the expletive omitted), then I feel an ache in my belly. If totally stuck, the ache rises up to my throat and I want to cry, then I sigh and cup my face in my hands. How about you?

Most people have more than one strategy. For me, when the ache begins in my belly there's a choice point. Rather than doing the 'cup my face in my hands' thing, I can clench my hands, shout 'Right!' in my head and refocus on the task with greater energy and enthusiasm. Or it can go another way, where the aching and head-holding are accompanied by more and more sighing and a running commentary in my head which says, 'I just can't do it … it's too much'. If I fail to notice that I'm adopting this strategy, I will certainly cave in and give up.

Being stuck, then, can be thought of as a state which consists of a pattern of thoughts, feelings and behaviours. It's something we do in response to a trigger and, crucially, it can quickly become a habitual pattern of response. In D&T the trigger for children might be 'not knowing' – for example, not knowing what to do next, what material or equipment to use, how to use a tool or technique or how to perform a skill. There are ample opportunities in D&T to encounter and identify triggers for getting into a stuck state. Consequently, there are ample opportunities to develop ways to move through and beyond stuck.

For children to develop resourceful responses to being in a stuck state they need to realise that they are in one. So in class we talk about what happens when you are stuck. I might say:

> Something you can do when you get stuck like this is to notice it. If you experience it as a feeling, for instance, notice your feeling ... notice what kind of feeling ... whereabouts. And you can ask yourself the questions – And is there anything else about (...)? And what kind of (...)? – so you can notice what it's like specifically.

> And remember that it's perfectly OK – it's part of learning. It's common to be stuck at some point when you are designing something. On the other hand, not everybody gets stuck and not everybody gets stuck every time, but it's quite common. Your feeling may change as you are noticing it or you may realise what else needs to happen for you to become unstuck.

During the making phase of a D&T task, I give minimal practical support for children's design ideas and their making. I focus on the learning dialogue and I facilitate children as they model their stuck state. There is usually insufficient time to talk with each child but open conversations with individuals, witnessed by either a group or the whole class, can help to raise awareness so the whole class come to realise that being stuck is a state they can recognise, name and learn to manage. Being stuck is not the end of learning and it's not something to be avoided and escaped from. It's a natural and important part of the learning process.

Here is an example of a quick conversation on the topic during a busy 'making' session. Matt had ground to a halt. He had run out of ideas and didn't know what to do next and said his mind had closed down.

| | |
|---|---|
| Me: | If nothing changes, what can you do to open your mind up again to good ideas? |
| Matt: | Imagine. |
| Me: | Ahh, imagine ... and is there anything else? |
| Matt: | Saying YES! |
| Me: | Ahh ... YES! ... and is there anything else that you can do to help yourself? |
| Matt: | Hmmm ... (*smiling*) ... |

Me:    OK ... so this is a time for you to notice and see what does help. What helps you move past stuck? Afterwards we'll talk about it and see what you have discovered – what helps you move past stuck?

In this example, Matt went on to notice what happens when he feels stuck and shared it with the class. The children then compared this to their own experience and shared similarities and differences, including the ways they had found to help themselves when stuck and to move beyond it.

Obviously, a single interaction like this one will have limited impact, but conversations like this do raise awareness. And when these kinds of conversations are drip-fed into lessons on a regular basis that awareness grows. When awareness grows children begin to experience being stuck as just a state they may pass through on their journey towards an outcome. When they can do this being stuck is no longer disabling for them. Stuck holds no fear.

In time, children learn to be much more comfortable, excited even, when they find themselves at a dead end. And when children know that being stuck is part of learning, rather than a sign of failure, they can relax and be curious, take risks and be creative.

## Meeting with failure

Thus far I've used the vehicle of D&T lessons as a means to address stuckness because D&T offers so many opportunities to address the issue. The projects lend themselves to making more than one attempt at something, so children can work through problems, explore possibilities, try different ways and succeed in the end.

It's important that children end on a good note in the early days, but it's also valuable for them to explore what happens when they don't succeed. When children are given opportunities to meet with failure and are facilitated with Clean Language to reflect on failures, in the same way as they do with other learning challenges (e.g. stuckness), they generate personalised, resourceful responses, such as self-management and taking responsibility. When children develop their own ways of responding resourcefully as they meet with challenges, they begin to generalise a level of awareness and resourcefulness in other subjects too – they become active and resilient learners.

(You can read more about using Clean Language in the D&T curriculum in a Cambridgeshire secondary school in Chapter 11.)

# Chapter 18

# Art

Attention is not in itself such an automatic process as you might presume. To make it work, it has to be activated, and if not, the opportunity to learn slips past.

John Hattie and Gregory Yates, *Visible Learning and the Science of How We Learn* (2013)

## Directing attention and noticing what's there

Years ago something happened that made me sit up and think about how I teach children to observe. I was wandering along a school corridor when I heard a teacher's voice through an open classroom door. The teacher inside was correcting a child, 'No, it's supposed to be realistic ... your river is brown. When have you ever seen a river that colour?' She added, 'Water is blue, not brown. Paint it again and make it blue this time.'

I ambled to the staffroom for a drink, reflecting on what I had just heard and recalling the rivers I had seen – realising that nearly every one of them is brown of one shade or another (mixed with hints of other colours and glints of reflected white light). I tried hard to recall if I had ever seen a blue river and to be honest I never had. I began to picture in my mind's eye the river that runs through our village. It's brown ... mostly.

(It reminded me of a moment in my childhood when, standing with my dad at the ocean's edge, we gazed towards the horizon and he asked with a puzzled tone, 'Where does it stop being sea and become sky?' I peered closely and pointed to the line where the sky meets the sea (thinking he couldn't see it). 'How do you know?' he replied. 'Because the colour changes from dark grey to light grey – just there – see?' It did change from dark grey to light grey. I declared, 'My teacher says the sky is blue but it's not blue is it – look!')

For the next week or so I noticed the sky and its changing colours ranging from nearly black to nearly white with all the colours of the rainbow in between. I recalled countless trips with my husband to fishing lakes where the water is brown or deep charcoal, and the seaside at Margate and Folkestone where I'd played as a child and where the sea sometimes shone pewter.

I thought about pictures in holiday brochures of azure or bright green water and Monet's paintings. What would Monet have to say if we asked him the colour of water? Or David Hockney – would he agree? And what about Van Gogh? In the staffroom I noticed the colours glistening in the tap water as I filled my glass …

Months later, when I asked the children in my class to draw their house, one boy coloured his a rich bright purple. We live in a village where the medieval houses come in shades of muted pink, yellow, green and cream. When I saw his purple house in the picture, I was inclined to correct him. I grew up among houses made of brick – houses aren't bright purple. Luckily, I stopped myself from telling him he was wrong. I remembered that here the houses may be any 'heritage' shade, but certainly not bright purple.

Sometimes children choose their favourite colour, or whatever colour catches their eye, or sometimes whichever pencil doesn't need sharpening, or sometimes whichever pencil *does* need sharpening (some make a career of sharpening). Knowing all that, I encouraged him to think again about his picture and to colour it the actual colour of his house. He insisted he wanted it purple, so short of time and keen to avoid a scene, I conceded and let him keep his purple house. Later that week, I drove past his newly painted, bright purple house.

These experiences have helped me to realise that when we share what we've learned we can be passing on distorted information, as in the game of Chinese whispers. And once a child takes on that information it will skew how they perceive the world. Children have assimilated such a lot before they even come to school that their eyes can already be closed to what is actually there. Take a simple banana, for instance. Most children will tell you that a banana is yellow, *fact*. If you ask them to draw a banana, most children will be able to draw one and they will colour it yellow.

If a child draws a banana *knowing* that bananas are yellow, they may just draw it and colour it yellow without paying attention to the detail. It is quite usual for them to draw what is in their head rather than what is actually there.

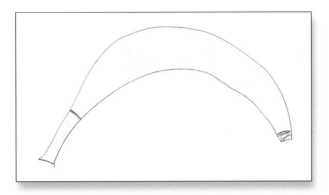

I began to wonder how I could guide the children to notice what is there in front of their eyes rather than in their mind's eye. Through observational drawing, children learn to look and see what is there, not what they think is there, which can be a valuable discipline for all areas of the curriculum.

I started to teach children to use their 'artist's eyes'. For this, children squint a little and peer through their eyelashes. Objects appear slightly blurred but they can see more clearly the shape, the colours, the lights and darks. I ask them to look ... and then look ... and then look ... and *then* draw (they should look at least three times before they draw once). When children use this technique to draw they notice so much more and their drawings are richer in observed detail.

But there are two problems with this approach. First, although looking through the haze of their eyelashes helps children to distinguish size and shape and contrasts in tone and shade, the details are blurred. And second, although looking with artist's eyes usefully slows them down – holding up their drawing long enough to afford them an opportunity to see what is there – it can't *make* them see.

Those of you who have ever tried to teach a young child to look both ways before crossing a road will be familiar with a kind of 'looking that does not see': children turn their heads and point their eyes in the right direction but still don't attend to the traffic – their minds are somewhere else. They are focusing on the head-turning instead of the traffic-spotting.

So how can you influence them to see? Something reinforced strongly in my training as a coach was the power of a question. Questions are attractive – they catch attention and seduce our minds to go in search of an answer. Clean questions offer an excellent way to direct children's attention. They offer a framework to direct attention systematically so that children notice more.

Looking three times using artist's eyes improves children's drawing, but when they use DDQs (e.g. 'And is there anything else about yellow?', 'And what kind of brown?', 'And whereabouts shiny?', 'And does shadow have a shape or a size?') they notice much more.

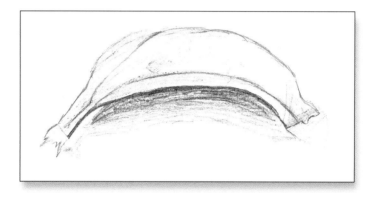

Clean questions direct and focus children's attention on the object they are observing and they consistently notice more than they do without the questions. It's hard for them *not* to notice more as they respond to the questions. And it's hard for them *not* to respond to the questions. The questions train their attention on specific attributes and they realise more of what is there.

I'm glad I took the walk along the corridor that day. Over the years I've noticed that British seas and rivers are almost never blue, and I've reflected on how our own beliefs and the conditioning we're subject to from those around us can override so easily what we see with our own eyes.

I'm also glad to be reminded of how important it can be to encourage children to be aware of what they perceive with their own senses and to know that their own first-hand experience is valid. When children have faith in themselves to see with their own eyes, to interpret the world from their own authentic experience, the scene is set for generative learning.

# Chapter 19

# PE

In PE children learn to use their bodies increasingly skilfully and they learn *through* their bodies (they acquire a feel for balance, force, momentum, space, rhythm, etc.) and *with* their bodies. Neuroscience and research into embodied cognition presents increasing evidence that information is held in our bodies as well as in our brains (see e.g. Williams and Bargh, 2008; Eerland et al., 2011).

One application of Clean Language in PE is the modelling of skills. Clean Language can be used to reveal what is involved in the performance of a skill so that other children can take it on board and use it in their own performance. Symbolic Modelling can help to elicit and transfer complex information that may be difficult to express in discrete 'bit by bit' detail (see Chapter 5).

Clean Language facilitation helps children learn through their own experience by focusing their attention on aspects of performance and facilitating reflection on their observations.

## Clean gymnastics

Marian Way is an established and well-respected Clean Language facilitator and trainer who started her working life as a teacher. Naturally, she was interested to learn how I was using Clean Language in the classroom, and a few years ago, after we had spoken on the phone a few times, we organised for her to visit my classroom. The children and I were excited and looking forward to her feedback. This is her account.

I've heard many tales of clean goings-on, but this was the first chance I got to see for myself how the children responded to clean questions (they call them the 'detail detective' questions). It was an action-packed day, with children both asking and answering the questions. This is what happened in the gym lesson.

Once the children were changed and in the hall, Julie reminded them of a metaphor they were already familiar with: that they should imagine having a 'string that reaches from the top of your head to the sky'. This got them all sitting up straight and was a great way of reminding them to have good posture throughout the lesson. Instead of nagging them to sit up straight, she simply said, 'Strings on.'

The lesson centred around the children creating sequences of stretching, balancing and travelling, on apparatus and floor mats. After they'd had a go, she talked them through a visualisation where they imagined themselves being on TV in a gymnastics competition, and they were to step into their TV self, and do their sequence again. Then came the 'clean' bit of the lesson: one child from each group performed their sequence while everyone else looked on. Julie asked the onlookers to notice for good quality movements and good ideas, and when the performers had finished she asked them what they noticed:

Child 1:  I liked A's balance.

Julie:  Oh you liked her balance. And what kind of balance was that?

Child 1:  Straight and tall.

Julie:  And is there anything else about that balance?

Child 1:  Yes, her head wasn't a bit wonky on its side. It was straight up.

Julie then asked A to repeat her sequence, so that everyone could see what had been noticed.

This way of doing things meant the praise was coming from another child rather than the teacher. Julie trusted that they had enough knowledge about gymnastics to be able to recognise a good move when they saw one. And by having the child show everyone the move again, they all got a chance to learn what a 'good' move looked like and to associate it with words like 'straight and tall'. So they were learning from each other, rather than from the 'expert'. And since the children's own words were used, there was also no chance of Julie using words that the children wouldn't understand.

Here are a couple more examples:

Child 2:   I liked B's jump.

Julie:   What kind of jump was that?

Child 2:   She did it straight like a pencil jump.

Child 3:   I liked C's forward roll.

Julie:   And you liked his forward roll. And is there anything else about that forward roll?

Child 3:   He did it in a kind of circle then went off and stood up at the end.

After a few of these short dialogues (each followed by a repeat performance), the questions started to become unnecessary because the children realised they needed to explain their thinking, so ...

Child 4:   I thought D was very good because when she bounced on the bench she had her string on.

Child 5:   E was straight and at the right angle.

Then came this one:

Child 6:   C's roll was a bit good.

Julie:   Is there anything else about a bit good?

Child 6:   She was doing it beautiful.

Julie:   What kind of beautiful?

Child 6:   Very beautiful.

Child 7:   If it was a bit good, what could she do to make it a bit gooder?

Child 6:   She could tuck her legs in.

Again, Julie stayed clean, and after a few exchanges another child, who'd picked up on the assumption in the original statement that there was room for improvement, asked a clean-ish question in the spirit of enquiry to help the performer know how it could be improved.

After this 'clean interlude' in the lesson, Julie asked everyone to run through in their minds what they had learned about really good moves and to see if they could incorporate it in their work. And off they went, striving to make the best moves they could in their sequences. I am no expert in gymnastics but I could see a big improvement between the children's first attempt and what they were doing by the end of the lesson. And Julie hadn't given them a single instruction about how to move, or singled out any child as being a model to watch. They had done it all by themselves.

# Chapter 20
# Music

Ruth Huckle is a dedicated music educator who adopts a 'music for all approach'. She is passionate about creating an environment that enables students to engage in learning to think and express themselves in their own way, empowering them to tap into the true potential within. She says, 'Using Clean Language in my multi-faceted work with students has opened up a whole new world and I constantly wonder at the treasure that is before me.' Ruth has shared her experiences with me over the past couple of years and she has generously agreed to share the following extract with you.

## The emperor

A really exciting moment occurred during a piano lesson with Alfie (10). He was playing a contrary motion scale in C major. Three notes in, with his left hand on A and his right hand on E, he suddenly became very animated and excited. He sounded them out in different octave ranges and eventually settled on A (first space bass clef and E, third space).

I stood back, allowing him time to explore his curiosity, then asked:

Ruth:    What's happening now?

Alfie:   It's that sound.

Ruth:    Is there anything else about that sound?

Alfie:   It's strong.

Ruth:    What kind of strong?

Alfie:   Powerful, strong.

Ruth:    And that's powerful and strong like what?

Alfie:   Like an emperor.

Ruth:    Whereabouts is that emperor?

Alfie:    High up, looking down on his people.

Ruth:    What kind of looking down?

Alfie:    Hmmm? Dominating. Is that the right word? You know, looking down. He's dominant and powerful.

I invited him to go home and draw a picture. He arrived at the next lesson with his emperor drawing sandwiched nicely between the pages in his music book.

The two notes he played (A and E) are the first (tonic) and the fifth (dominant) note of an A scale. He knew innately that a perfect fifth (the interval between A and E, tonic to dominant) is very powerful and pivotal. Now, when he hears any two notes like that, he can recognise them immediately and says, 'Oh, there's the "emperor" sound, the perfect fifth.' This sound completely captivated and inspired Alfie and he went on to write 'The Emperor' as a piano solo.

As Alfie was considering his composition, I used sequencing questions and the musical ideas kept emerging from him like little sparks. He knew exactly how he wanted it to sound! I helped him get it down on paper; everything else is his creation.

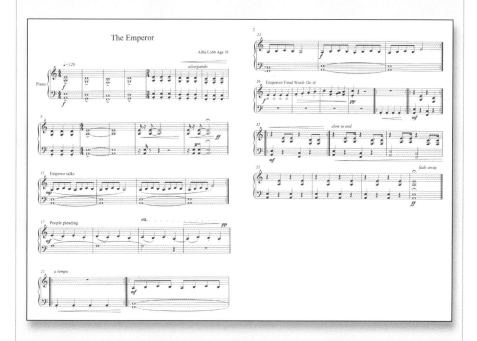

What happens next? Alfie is orchestrating this tune now and is full of ideas for new compositions. It has been truly wonderful to see Alfie discovering his inner musical world. This has utterly confirmed my long held belief that learning is 'sparked and sustained by curiosity'. He has since said, 'I didn't know I could do that!'

# Part 3
# Finding Their Own Way

# Chapter 21
# The Infants' Christmas Play

As Christmas approaches most of the infant teachers in the land are turning their attention to the Christmas play, and everything it involves begins to loom fairly large on the horizon. In our school it's no different. We generally put on two performances for parents in the last week of term, with each infant class contributing to the shared event (a dance, a song, a poem or a short play) to create a complete production. The infant teaching staff get together to coordinate it and ensure the amalgamated performance is a balanced one – so we don't end up with four dances, four poems or four plays.

Some years ago, at a regular infant staff meeting, a colleague broached the subject of the Christmas play for the first time that term. It's always an awesome moment when this happens because it heralds the start of the Christmas season – a kind of runaway juggernaut experience or roller coaster perhaps (choose your own intense, accelerating, careering dangerously out of control metaphor). There's often a smidge of Joyce Grenfell about it too!

One teacher says that her class will be doing a song and another has a dance in mind for her class. 'So will you do a play?' they ask. I know that if my class does opt for a play the whole production will be nicely balanced, so the obvious and easy answer (and probably the one that is expected of me) is 'Yes, of course.' But I haven't spoken with my class yet and if I go ahead and decide what they are going to do without their input, I'll be denying them the ownership that I want them to have. I know my answer won't be a popular one, 'I don't know, I haven't asked the children yet.'

Ignition ... Brrrrmm, brrrrmm growls the juggernaut. The brakes are off!

'That's very democratic,' they reply.

# Clean preparation

I usually ask the children in my class what they would like to do and get them involved in brainstorming ideas for our part of the performance. I don't give it a lot of thought personally until I've spoken with them because I want them to have as much ownership of it as possible. However, I'm acutely aware that it will take time to consult with the children ... and the juggernaut is already growling. Hmm.

At times like this it can seem far quicker and easier for me to plan the whole thing myself and then just tell the children what to do – it's a tempting option. But I wonder about the value of doing it that way. There is a large part of me that resists the easy option. (Sometimes I so wish that part of me would take a rest!)

The experience for the children needs to be as rich a learning experience as it can be. I want them to have as much input as possible to the planning and decision-making. But this can't be an open-ended free-for-all: there's a timescale, there are deadlines to be met and other people are depending on our contribution – and they want answers *now*.

I reflect for a while. The coach/facilitator in me knows that the situation is wonderfully suited to a clean approach. Clean facilitation offers a framework for the children to work freely with their own ideas. Using facilitation skills, I'll be able to move the process on in a timely fashion without interfering with the children's ideas for the content. I decide to approach the subject cleanly with the children the next day so that I can give my colleagues an answer.

I present my class with the following scenario so they have the context and a frame for the challenge:

> We (the infants) present a production to the parents at Christmas. It's a combined effort involving all infant classes. It usually includes dance, drama and music and is linked in some way to the nativity story. What-ever we do needs to blend in, in a balanced way, with the other class con-tributions. Two of the other classes have already chosen. One is doing a dance and one is doing a song. They need to know what we're going to do.

All I need to do now is ask them, 'And with all of that (referencing the frame) ... what would you like to have happen?' Simple. But instead I lose my nerve (I let go of my faith in the process, in my class and in myself) and I ask, 'Would you like to dance ... or sing ... or do a play?' The children fire back ideas and I summarise them, 'Oh, singing and dancing *and* a play. It will be a musical.' My inner voice (the inner control freak) barks at me, 'That'll teach you to ask them what they'd like!'

Continuing along in a directive way (rather than the facilitative way that I had planned) I announce, 'We'll need some kind of subject matter, some kind of story, and I don't know what that's going to be.' At times I pretend I don't know something in order to stimulate the children to think, but on this occasion I didn't know. So they began to look for an appropriate storybook and, coincidentally, the first book found had a tentative link with Christmas and seemed suitable for the task.

The story turned out to be a heart-warming tale about an old hare who feeds the birds. When it gets cold and wintery all the birds fly away, except a little robin who lives in a fir tree in the forest. The hare goes to the forest to feed her, but a terrible storm blows down the fir tree and he worries about the robin, fearing she's dead. He's happy when he hears her cheeping and realises she's alive. He drags her tree through the forest, sets it up as a home for her beside his burrow, and begins to feed her. She sings to him and he feels young again. They're happy ever after.

The children love it. 'Can that be our play, Miss?' 'Yes, it can.' And then I'm off into 'teacher mode' again, telling them what to do. 'If we're going to do this as a play, we need to pick out the characters; we need to be thinking what characters are in the story.'

There are only three characters in the story (including the tree). I didn't see how we could do it with 27 children in the class. But the children soon identified possibilities: there are trees, there's a flock of birds — we can do a bird dance, and there is a magical moon and the sun (the sun puts in a brief appearance at the end). Soon we have lots of characters and roles for a narrator or two.

The children chose their roles. They made a first, second and third choice, so that if they didn't land their first choice there was an alternative they could be happy with. As it happened, lots of children wanted to be birds and do a dance, so everyone was accommodated easily. Over the next few days I read the story to them a couple more times, and when it was time to create the play we went to the hall to begin.

# Clean creation

Everything seemed to be moving in the right direction, so I summoned up some faith (at last) to tackle the next part of the process cleanly.

> We have half an hour in here ... and we want to do our play ... so in this half hour what would you like to have happen?
>
> Can we go on the stage?
>
> Yes.

Some children start to be silly.

> Stop ... we've got half an hour ... and you want to do a play ... and what would you like to have happen?

The children go over to the stage and begin to discuss what to do.

I wondered what would happen if I only asked clean questions. I tried to hold a 'sense of knowing' that they *would* be able to do it without my constant direction. And after a short period of chaos, with everybody talking at once, three directors emerged with some good ideas. For example, one child wanted to be a narrator *and* a tree, and they figured out between them that his narrating role would have to occur later on in the play because he couldn't play two roles simultaneously. He would need to be a tree first and then reappear later, somewhere else, dressed differently for the narrator role. He would have to slip off the back of the stage and crawl under it to the front to take up his narrator's position, in a way that no one would notice.

And for the bird dance, they decided that six birds would dance in a circle formation, four in a square and three in a triangle, and they took on these formations – just like that. If you have ever tried to shepherd a group of young children into a particular formation, or even into a straight line, you will understand how impressed I was when I witnessed this. They could do it far better than when I help them. This was self-organisation in action.

I was not completely silent, but rather than deciding what would happen and directing the action, I stayed in the background as a resource for the children – keeping track of the time. Once everything was up and running, I spoke only four times:

- At one point, when a child complained to the birds, 'You keep coming across the stage without stopping,' I suggested he could ask them, 'What would you like to have happen?' instead. When he asked the question he discovered that the birds wanted to dance. They made square, triangle and circle formations and moved their arms with a graceful flying action and the whole thing developed from a stomp across the stage into a dance in a matter of seconds.

- I let them know when there were just five minutes to go and they quickly got up and did the bird dance again.

- When some children were dancing backwards towards the steps that led off the stage, I put my health and safety hat on and suggested they organise the dance so that they keep away from the steps.

- The trees found it hard to stay in one place so I explained that trees have roots.

Was I tempted to get in there and start directing? Yes, very much so. Some of the stronger characters in my class were growing in confidence, having good ideas and making particularly effective contributions. I monitored to ensure that others were having opportunities as well and to check the confident ones weren't bossing them around.

At one point they discussed the circle and triangle idea and three or four children spoke at once, telling the birds what to do – the birds were not having a say. A child came over to me to report, 'I think we're giving the birds a hard time.' (The birds actually looked like they were having a good time!) I responded, '... and you think you're giving the birds a hard time ... and when you think you're giving the birds a hard time, what needs to happen?' He thought for a while, returned to the group and suggested, 'Hey guys, let the birds have a say!'

Even the youngest children who didn't have any past experience of school productions to draw on were more engaged than those I've worked with in previous years. Children usually tend to daydream or chat during rehearsals and then miss their cues, and I have to keep reminding them what to do. This year, though, every single child was engaged and knew what to do and when. That had never happened before.

Yes, at times they were loud and I observed carefully from a distance, checking to see if I needed to intervene – I didn't want this to turn into a 'Lord of the Flies' kind of thing – but there were no behavioural problems. Usually in a play practice I'll be asking those who aren't involved in the immediate action to 'Please sit still and be quiet'. But there was no need – all the children were totally engaged, agreeing where everyone would be and how it would work.

Something that particularly impressed me was that many of the elements of storytelling they had been learning about in literacy lessons were apparent in the decisions they were making about the play. They used repetitive patterns in the dialogue to inject humour, repetition in the plot to fuel anticipation and suspense, and expressive and engaging vocabulary. I reflected this back to them afterwards in the form of clean feedback.

I told them that I could see structures and patterns in their play, such as the circle, the square and the triangle in the bird dance: 'I never would have thought of that. It was great.' And then they abandoned it because it was too complicated and because the stage wasn't big enough and because the trees were in the way.

I was so tempted to say that if the trees just moved an inch or two then the birds would have room, and that it wasn't too complicated, it was beautiful, it just needed a little more practice. But I held back and respected their decisions. I managed not to say anything, even when their new version with the birds flying only once through the trees before exiting seemed not nearly as clever to me.

I minimised my input with the costumes too. The previous year I had designed the costumes, obtained the cloth, cut it and made them. This year, we unpacked all the costumes stored from previous plays and together they decided what would be useful. There were plenty of old angel costumes which could be converted to bird costumes and some children took items home for their parents to work on.

I even resisted telling the parents exactly what to do – for example, for the robin I just said, 'Jenny has an old red costume and some brown material, and she needs to be a robin, thank you,' and trusted Jenny's mum to decide how to make that happen. And when the costume was finished it looked beautiful. So much so that the rest of the birds looked quite plain in comparison (in my opinion only – none of the children mentioned this). At the last minute I asked the other children if they would like to have a collar of feathers around their necks and I photocopied some feather shapes, which they coloured and added glitter to before we stuck them on a collar of card around their necks. There I went interfering again.

The children suggested the trees needed some branches so I agreed they could go outside and find some. During one of their rehearsal discussions the children said they needed leaves as well to blow from the branches in the storm. They looked outside at playtime but all the leaves were soggy and horrid, so they found a couple that weren't too distressed and asked me to photocopy them to make templates. The children then coloured them to make their own leafy props.

# Dress rehearsal

The next step was the first dress rehearsal. All the classes met in the hall and I was interested to see the other teachers telling their classes exactly what to do. It highlighted for me the difference in our approach this year.

One teacher was keen to devise and practise a seating plan so our class would file tidily back onto the stage for a song a few minutes after their play performance finished, but the children had already organised how they would get back on stage and had devised and memorised their positions independently. When I told her they had sorted it out themselves already she was understandably doubtful and was surprised when they sprang into action, right on cue.

As we went through the rehearsal, I stood aside, gazing away from my class because I didn't want to slip into my previous role – cuing them in throughout the performance. I wanted them to carry on with their self-reliant approach. They knew I trusted them to pull it off now.

Another teacher, noticing my inattention, wandered over to alert me quietly, 'It will soon be your class's turn on stage.' As I was explaining about our approach this year, that they had been working independently and would know themselves when to begin, they stood, moved onto the stage and began their performance with no cues at all. I continued to avert my gaze so they didn't look to me for direction and I said nothing while they performed.

I was mildly surprised that nobody said, 'Do you think you'll have this licked into shape in time?' but it didn't happen. To my colleagues observing it was obviously ready. In previous years I would be thinking about squeezing in some extra practice sessions at this point and other people would have agreed that we needed it. There was no need for it this time.

I intervened as a couple of other adults attempted to direct the children in response to the absence of direction from me. One of the teachers said, 'It would be better if the narrator moved nearer to the microphone and … ' I interrupted her and quietly explained our new method, so she understood why we weren't inviting her advice. In retrospect I realise it might have been prudent to brief the other staff on the nature of our approach that year, but as I wanted everything else about the production to unfold in its usual way I had decided against announcing it in advance.

My teaching assistant was well-versed in the benefits of a clean approach and had already used Clean Language to facilitate children's learning in class, but she too had to resist the urge to step in and help as we prepared for the performance. It was extremely difficult for her to stand back and allow the children to take responsibility to the extent we were aiming for. I had to repeatedly remind her not to fold up the costumes after every performance – helping can be a habit.

When you find your role is to do next to nothing, it can be difficult to know what to do. On the afternoon of the first dress rehearsal, a parent popped in to sew the last of the leaves on to the tree costumes and she watched the first part of the rehearsal. She was impressed. She said, 'It must be hard work for you.' I couldn't take the credit. I told her the truth: 'Interestingly enough, the children have done it all themselves. I've given them the time and space and they have done it themselves.'

Despite the success to this point, I still didn't know if I could continue in a purely facilitative role right through to the final performance. I felt nervous. Was I doing the right thing? I had never let go of the reins so completely before. My hypothesis was that it would be easier for everyone and that we would get a better result, but it was important to monitor whether this was true.

I certainly didn't want to be spurred along by my enthusiasm for a clean and emergent approach in an indulgent way. I wasn't about to let the children down, so I decided to get some feedback from the children and to keep a wary eye on the quality of the work myself, standing poised to take command if necessary.

# Feedback

Just before the final dress rehearsal I invited the children to notice what they were noticing during the performance, because afterwards we would talk about what they had noticed. And when we came back to the classroom afterwards, I said, 'We've done a practice and you noticed what you noticed … and so talk to a partner about what you noticed.' I gave them just a few minutes to do this and then asked what they had noticed. Their responses included:

I didn't believe in the characters.

The trees were moving around the stage instead of rooted to the spot.

The moon was chattering to the trees.

The narrators were discussing things.

The narrator who changed from a tree to a narrator – when the tree was blown down, he crawled like a commando and I hope nobody noticed him.

Crawling narrator … lying on stage and rolling around.

At the end … somebody said very loudly, 'The end'.

When somebody put forward an opinion like, 'I didn't believe in the characters', I wanted to see if this was a general view or an isolated opinion. So I repeated it: 'Oh, so you didn't believe in the characters. Did anyone else feel like that?' It was clear that a lot of the children didn't believe in the characters. I asked, 'So what needs to happen next?'

The narrator should speak louder or sit nearer the microphone.

The birds need to move their wings clearly and boldly.

The birds should slow down, and walk like they're looking at something really interesting and dance floating.

The birds need to cheep 'goodbye' louder.

The birds need to look where they're putting their hands. They should be ready to go and keep awake.

The birds need to get their partners before they go on the stage.

The narrators need to talk louder, sweeter, bolder and clearer. They need to check their bookmarks are in place. (One child said he would be responsible for checking this.)

I think it's best if we do not look at our parents ... we will go out of our mind. So look at your partner and do what you're doing.

Some of these suggestions led to improvements the next time they rehearsed the play. Then we shared feedback again and gathered more suggestions, and their performance improved further still.

# Performance and reflection

I simply stood at the back throughout the final performances. With my 'keep out of the way' hat on, I couldn't help but consider just how much I must have been 'in the way' in the past. Previously, I would shepherd the children around the stage or even stand behind the audience and make hand signals to direct them.

This year the children were able to cue themselves in. They could do this because they had full ownership of their work. And because they trusted that I wouldn't step in or bail them out, they were able to take on the responsibility themselves.

When we were back in the classroom after the last performance, we shared some feedback:

The trees stood still.

The tree-narrator went under the stage well.

The hare looked like he believed in himself.

The birds did the dance.

The birds tweeted well.

The moon was good.

Then I gave the children a clap and said, 'Well done team! *You* made this up, *you* decided what to do, *you* practised, *you* fed back, improved – practised, fed back, improved – and *you* performed. And that was your final performance ... and with all of that ... what do you know now? ... and put that down on paper.' I wanted to see what would happen.

This is what they wrote:

I know I was standing still. I standed still and noticed I was standing still and didn't get told off.

I know I'm getting greater.

I know I can make up my own show.

I know I didn't see the tree/narrator crawl under the table, but I don't think he should be a narrator. (Meaning, he shouldn't have two parts.)

I know I was very good at standing still as a moon.

I know I am very good at standing still as a tree.

I know I am really good.

I know now I think the birds were really good.

I think I was a lot more confident and better.

I know I can stand in front of the people really well. (This was a child who was previously afraid.)

I know I can stand real still and sit real still. (Referring to the times when he wasn't on stage.)

I know I can sing in front of all the parents.

I believed I was a real narrator and can read hard stories. (This child's reading level was particularly low at the start of the project. He practised diligently to read his contribution well. An unintended outcome was that his reading level and motivation to read – beyond the play – shot up during the course of the project.)

I felt like a real bird in the sky, flying.

I know now to believe in myself.

I feeled as if I was a real tree and I would like to be a tree.

I noticed I was being really confident.

I know that the tree/narrator can get behind the burrow without being seen.

I know I am more confident.

What I also noticed was that the play evolved and changed in a natural way. Sometimes a play becomes stiff, there's no ad-libbing, and so if something goes wrong the others don't know what to do. This year the children were more able to ad-lib and to work around anything that went wrong. In the first performance, for example, the burrow fell off the stage but the show just went on.

Then I gave *myself* a clap and said, 'Well done ... phew! ... and with all of that ... what do I know now? ... and put that down on paper.'

This is what I wrote. I know ...

- I have a responsibility to the children to create the conditions whereby they can learn and do their best.

- There are expectations from the parents, the school and from colleagues to come up with the goods and I didn't want to let the children down.

- I sensed a tension between taking a sure and safe path with a clearly defined ending and going off-piste.

- As a facilitator and coach I'm familiar with working in unknown territory and I know that learning and growth arises from it.

- As a teacher my confidence waxed and waned throughout the project.

- The children were engaging in valuable learning in multiple areas and at multiple levels.

- I was scared to relinquish control because:

  > I was unsure what the outcome would be.

  > I was unsure where to go next.

  > I was unsure that I would be able to justify it to my colleagues' satisfaction, if they had asked what we were doing (although, of course, I could have asked the children to provide that information).

- I took a leap of faith to see it through and I called on past experiences in teaching, coaching and facilitating where working in unknown territory like this, although uncomfortable, had been successful and productive.

- Clean principles gave me bearings so I knew I was never lost at sea, even when the land was out of sight.

- At all times I was free and able to take the rudder and control the direction if, at any time, it became necessary.

- It was worthwhile.

- It was a success – based on the children's, parents', colleagues' and my own feedback.

# Chapter 22
# Young Explorers

## Setting up a project group

A group of 7 and 8-year-olds wanted to find out more about the DDQs and how they could use them to enhance their learning, so we convened a small research and development group. At our first meeting the children explored boundaries and set ways of working together which were agreed by everyone in the group. I used a clean approach to facilitate the meeting, loosely based on the Clean Set Up process developed by Dee Berridge and Caitlin Walker.[1]

The meeting began with a lot of disorganised shouting and collecting of laptops in preparation for something ... for what? I'm not sure because nothing had yet been discussed. The rest of the class were making their way to the hall for assembly. There was a lot of excited enthusiasm in the group.

You will see two distinct phases in the questioning transcribed below. The frame for the first phase of the process was a focus on how the *group* needed to be and the second phase focused on how the *individuals* needed to be.

In preparation for the first phase I stuck some large sheets of flip-chart paper on the wall for recording our thoughts and wrote, 'For this group to work at its best, it needs to be like what?' I asked the question of children in turn and wrote their contributions on the paper.

(Note: For brevity, in the transcript below I've used the word 'repeat' in brackets wherever I repeated back the child's words verbatim, using the syntax of Clean Language questioning – see Chapter 3.)

---

1   See Walker (2014), p. 30.

# First child

John:    For Jeni to stop being like standing up and telling everybody what to do because (*looking at Jeni*) you are making everybody be a bit hyper and start shouting at you.

Me:    And when that happens, and Jeni does stop, then what happens?

John:    It will be a calmer group and we will be able to have a better system.

Me:    (*repeat*) And when (*repeat*) then what happens?

John:    The group will be perfect.

Me:    (*repeat*) And what kind of group would that group be, when it is perfect like that?

John:    It will be an amazing group where we would use our ideas.

Me:    (*repeat*) Anything else?

John:    No. It will be an amazing group where we would use our ideas.

Me:    Thank you.

# Second child

Me:    And for this group to work at its best, it needs to be like what?

David:    We need to share and be peaceful.

Me:    (*repeat*) And when share and be peaceful, what kind of share?

David:    Taking turns.

Me:    (*repeat*) And is there anything else about share?

David:    No one gets left out.

Me:    (*repeat*) And anything else about share?

David:    No.

| | |
|---|---|
| Me: | And we need to share like that, take it in turns, no one gets left out ... and be peaceful. And what kind of peaceful? |
| David: | Quiet ... you have nobody shouting at you ... a bit like now. |
| Me: | (*repeat*) |
| Another child: | Because everyone's listening and taking their time. Because everyone's listening ... and taking thoughts in, taking their thoughts in. |
| Me: | (*repeat*) Thank you. |

# Third child

| | |
|---|---|
| Lynn: | We all give in our ideas and make sure that nobody's shy and we all get our ideas through. |
| Me: | (*repeat*) And when all that ... and we all give in our ideas ... what kind of 'give in', when we all give in our ideas? |
| Lynn: | Well, we need to make sure that everybody hears it and it gets put down on a piece of paper, like everybody else's idea ... or in a book really. |
| Me: | (*repeat*) And what kind of through ... when you give in your ideas ... what kind of through? |
| Lynn: | Well, exactly the same as 'give in' really. |
| Me: | (*repeat*) And make it sure ... what kind of sure? |
| Lynn: | Well, they're definitely happy (*looking around the group*). |
| Me: | (*repeat*) And as I'm writing on a piece of paper now, it's happening now I suppose? |
| Lynn: | Oh yeah! Well, yeah instantly! |
| Me: | Two things have come up that are actually happening now: there's the 'put down on a piece of paper' that's happening now and the 'share and be peaceful'. |
| Lynn: | Yeah. |
| Me: | And you have another one, you said? |
| Lynn: | No. |
| Me: | Thank you. |

# Fourth child

| | |
|---|---|
| Steve: | Um ... Jeni ... needs to stop being a bossy boots ... exclamation mark, exclamation mark, exclamation mark, exclamation mark, exclamation mark ... OK, a few more of them, one, two, three, four, five, six, seven, eight, nine ... and a picture that Jeni really does *not* need to see. |
| Me: | (*repeat*) And when all of that ... then what happens? |
| Steve: | Well, then (a) I might like Jeni a bit more and (b) the group will be a bit better. |
| Me: | (*repeat*) And when, like Jeni a bit more *and* the group is a bit better ... then what happens? |
| Steve: | Um, well, I'll like Jeni a bit more so I'll listen to her ideas more ... and also the group will be better so we can learn more from her ideas. |
| Me: | (*repeat*) And when listen to her ideas a bit more ... what kind of listening will that be? |
| Steve: | Well, actually taking it all in. Because I did remember in the past that if somebody I don't like says it, I kind of forget about it and then discuss other ideas that me and my friends think ... so I kind of like say 'your idea doesn't count'. ... It's a bit immature really. |
| Me: | (*repeat*) And when, let's think ... and when 'a bit immature really' ... is there anything else about that? |
| Steve: | Well, it's just a bit silly really ... Hmm, everybody has fantastic ideas ... and just to rule them out because you don't like them socially ... so you can't learn from them ... it's a bit stupid really. |
| Me: | (*repeat*) Hmm ... and knowing all of that ... and we all give in our ideas ... and make sure that nobody's shy and we all get our ideas through ... is there anything else about that? |
| Steve: | Well, then we can learn more. |
| Me: | (*repeat*) And is there anything else that needs to go on here? |

Steve:      Hmm ... well, not really, no.

Me:         OK, thank you.

# Fifth child

Nicola:     To be friendly with each other.

Me:         ... and is there anything else about friendly?

Nicola:     Just friendly.

Me:         ... and as I write this ... is there anything else?

Nicola:     Just to be friendly.

Me:         OK, thank you.

# Sixth child

Jodie:      To join in and have fun.

Me:         (*repeat*) ... and is there anything else about join in?

Jodie:      Hmm ...

Me:         Hmm ... what kind of join in?

Jodie:      Like ... well like ... everyone coming ... like us all being here.

Me:         (*repeat*)

Jodie:      In our group for everyone to listen ... and that everyone has a turn to be speaking and no one to be bossy, and to show one another their thoughts ... and for everybody to be nice.

Me:         (*repeat*) ... and when all that happens ... that's like what ... what's that like?

Jodie:      We're a happier group and we be much quieter ... I thought it would be happier if we go round in a circle with no people keeping interrupting ... and we go round in a circle like we are now ... for everybody to get out their thoughts.

Me:         (*repeat*) Thank you.

# Seventh child

| | |
|---|---|
| Katie: | I would like our group to listen to everyone, to share ideas and be friendly towards each other. |
| Me: | (*repeat*) ... and when listen like that ... what kind of listen? |
| Katie: | Listen so you've got it in your head and you take in the information. |
| Me: | (*repeat*) ... and what kind of share, when you share ideas? |
| Katie: | You share them and so you let your ideas out and you let other people hear them. |
| Me: | (*repeat*) ... and be friendly towards each other ... and what kind of friendly? |
| Katie: | Friendly where it's not necessarily that you have to be best friends but you're kind to them. |
| Me: | (*repeat*) |
| Katie: | For Steve to stop being horrid. |
| Me: | ... and when Steve stops being horrid ... then what happens? |
| Katie: | He's a little bit more better behaved towards other people. |
| Me: | ... and when he's a little bit more better behaved towards other people ... then what happens? |
| Katie: | He gets more friends and he's a bit more happy. |
| Me: | (*repeat*) ... and then what happens? |
| Katie: | He stops being nasty. |
| Me: | And when he stops being nasty ... then what happens? |
| Katie: | When he stops being nasty everybody's happy. |
| Me: | And when everybody's happy ... then what happens? |
| Katie: | It's a better environment to be taught in. |

# Eighth child

| | |
|---|---|
| Jack: | We should all just … people get on together. |
| Me: | Anything else? |
| Jack: | Like whatever anybody else is saying … only JMC [Mrs McCracken] should be able to tell us what to do. |
| Me: | (*repeat*) … and what kind of 'get on' is that get on? |
| Jack: | Not really like friends … but just be nice. |
| Me: | (*repeat*) … and if I'm the only one allowed to tell you what to do … then what happens? |
| Jack: | Then you're to be just like one person … because you tell us to work it out and decide together. |
| Me: | (*repeat*) … and is there anything else? |
| Jack: | (*shakes his head*) |

# Ninth child

| | |
|---|---|
| Sue: | When like … if it's like *you're* talking or someone else is talking, everyone like needs to be listening … and not like shouting out, just take their turn … so like be patient … and wait until *their* turn is theirs, then they can do, then they can think what they want. |
| Me: | (*repeat*) |
| Sue: | Yeah, and you should take turns like one person get the laptop each week. |

Then I summarised for them in their own words:

| | |
|---|---|
| Me: | So let's see what we've got here … (*gathering together and displaying flip-chart sheet notes*). For this group to be work-ing at its best it needs to be an amazing group where we use our ideas. And we need to share – take it in turns so nobody gets left out. And be peaceful – that's quiet peace-ful, with nobody shouting at you – everybody listening and |

taking thoughts in. It needs to be that we all give in our ideas – that is, make sure everybody hears it and it gets put down on a piece of paper. And make sure that we all get our ideas through and learn from each other and that it definitely happens. We need to be friendly with each other and join in and have fun. It'll be a happier group if we go round in a circle, for everybody to get their ideas through. And we need to listen – take the information in – listen to everyone. To share ideas and be friendly so that everybody has a chance to hear. It's not necessary that you have to be best friends but we're kind to each other ... and it's a better environment to be taught in. And people to get on – not really like friends but just nice – to get on together. And that only JMC should be able to tell us what to do because JMC helps us decide together.

And thinking on those things ... and with all of that ... is there anything else?

| | |
|---|---|
| Jack: | For this group to work at its best it needs to be divided into groups and we all have different areas or jobs. |
| Me: | (*repeat*) And is there anything else? |
| Jack: | No. |
| Me: | Thank you. |

Then I changed tack. I moved the frame from a focus on how the group needs to be to how individuals need to be. I wanted each of them to consider their own role in this group, so I sent them off to think on this and to write/draw 'what they need to be like':

So ... what I'd like you to go away and do quite quickly is ... I'd like you to think about ... 'And for this group to work at its best like that, *I* need to be like what?'

So go quietly and take a piece of paper and in your own mind ... jot down what *you* need to be like for this group to be at its best, just like that (*gesturing to description of the group displayed on the flip-chart paper*).

The children moved to desks or other spaces in the room and wrote and/or drew their responses.

## Working together as a team

Later we shared what they had drawn or written. In this way everyone had a good idea of what everyone else thought about their role in the group and the contribution they would make to it. This led to them forming subgroups with specific job roles.

These children were able to go on to work together with a professional approach. They knew, understood and bought into the boundaries and the structure of the group, which meant the time it took to establish 'the rules' was recovered many times over during the course of our work together. The management of the group was a walk in the park as the group was self-organised.

This group went on to independently explore the role of DDQs in their learning and thinking, devise an introduction to DDQs for other children, produce a PowerPoint presentation on the subject and present it to a class of 9 and 10-year-olds.

## Self-organising

This way of working affords each participant the opportunity to input on how the group will operate so their needs are met. This approach works well in whole-class contexts for building self-organising learning teams (see Chapters 4 and 7). It also creates conditions for group members to view situations from multiple perspectives: from their own perspective, from that of other individuals and from the perspective of the group as a whole. In this way they become experienced at taking others' needs and the needs of the group into account.

When they generate the rules like this there's wriggle room: they can refine the rules as they learn more about each other and as the community of learners grows and develops. This is an organic and responsive process rather than (as are many rules-based systems) a rigid and fixed procedure.

## But what if somebody breaks the rules?

Rule-breaking is a signal to the group to explore what needs to happen. It may be a sign that the rules need to be refined. It may be that an individual realises (as in the transcript above) that their perspective needs to change. An individual may decide to leave the group. The key point here is that *they* decide.

## Conclusion
# And What Would You Like to Have Happen Now?

A hundred children, a hundred individuals who are people – not people-to-be, not people of tomorrow, but people now, right now – today.

Janusz Korczak, *How To Love a Child* (1920)


## What just happened?

Children finding their own way ...

    exploring ways to facilitate self-directed learning in the curriculum ...

      modelling thinking ...

        metaphor the foundation of thought ...

          asking Clean Language questions ...

            David Grove developing clean questions ...

and those 5, 6 and 7-year-old children in that mixed-age infant classroom ... and me wondering what happens next?


## And what do I know now?

Throughout history childhood has been created by the social discourse of the age: in Victorian times children climbed chimneys; in my own preschool years we were put to work on farms in a way that would breech child labour laws today (I loved every minute of it!); now, in the UK, children increasingly remain dependent on parental support, sometimes until they are in their thirties.

Beliefs, values, knowledge and understanding changes throughout time and across cultures and influences our expectations for our children – we create collective expectations and we instil limitations around children as we do it. When raising standards is so high on the educational agenda, perhaps it's time to consider the extent to which what limits our children is *our* view of what they are capable of.

I know that young children can have thoughts as big and profound as those of adults. They have the sensibilities but not necessarily the words to articulate them just yet. Alison Gopnik's (2010) research shows that babies think as scientists (i.e. generating hypotheses and testing them) and that by the age of 18 months children have developed a 'theory of mind' – babies can appreciate that other people may believe different things, or want different things, to them and they can see situations from another person's perspective and modify their behaviour accordingly.

A 7-year-old who had been exposed to Clean Language questions for around two terms had been pondering and wondering about this and that for a while before rushing excitedly to explain his thinking: 'Mrs McCracken ... when you stop to think about it ... everything is ... well ... it's all ... well ... really, when you think about it ... the basic elements of *everything* ... is ... time ... or ... space!'

## What happens next?

My challenge now is to continue to facilitate learning, taking great care to keep out of children's way as they engage warp speed, respecting and witnessing their undoubted wisdom and trusting them to step boldly into a future that they alone can create – and trusting they can do it. As John Holt (1964: 283) observes: 'Since we cannot know what knowledge will be most needed in the future, it is senseless to try to teach in advance. Instead, we should try to turn out people who love learning so much and learn so well that they will be able to learn whatever needs to be learned.'

## Practice task (write and/or draw your responses)

- And with all of that ... what do *you* know now?

- And is there anything else you know now?

- And what difference does that knowing make?

- And what will you do differently now as a result?

- And what is a first action that you could take?

- And can that happen?

- And will that happen?

And take all the time you need to consider what you would like to have happen now, and in the days and weeks to follow, as you continue to create conditions for you and the children in your care to flourish.

# Pocket-Sized Question Card

**Clean Language Questions**

And is there anything else/anything else about (...)?

And what kind of (...)?

And where/whereabouts is (...)?

And what happens next?

And then what happens?

And what happens just before?

And where does/could (...) come from?

And is there a relationship between ( ... ) and ( ... )?

And when ( ... ), what happens to ( ... )?

And that's like what?

And what would you/( ... ) like to have happen?

And what needs to happen for (desired outcome)?

And can that ( ... ) happen?

# Detail Detective Question
# Magnifying Glass

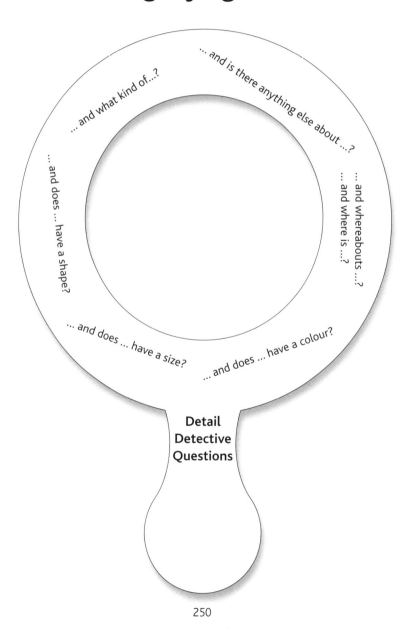

... and what kind of...?

... and is there anything else about ...?

... and does ... have a shape?

... and whereabouts ...?
... and where is ...?

... and does ... have a size?

... and does ... have a colour?

**Detail
Detective
Questions**

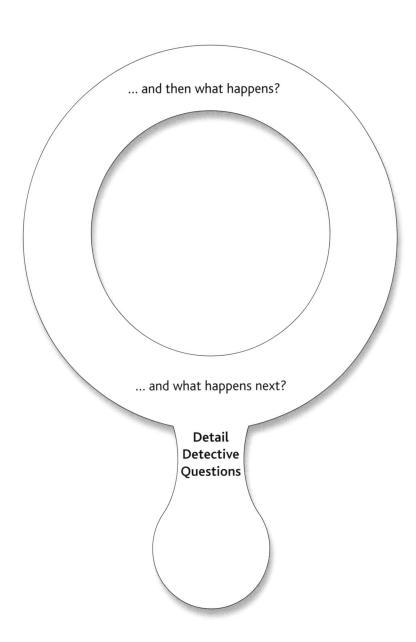

... and then what happens?

... and what happens next?

**Detail
Detective
Questions**

# Appendix C
# Story Direction Cards

# Appendix D
# Detail Detective Question Fan

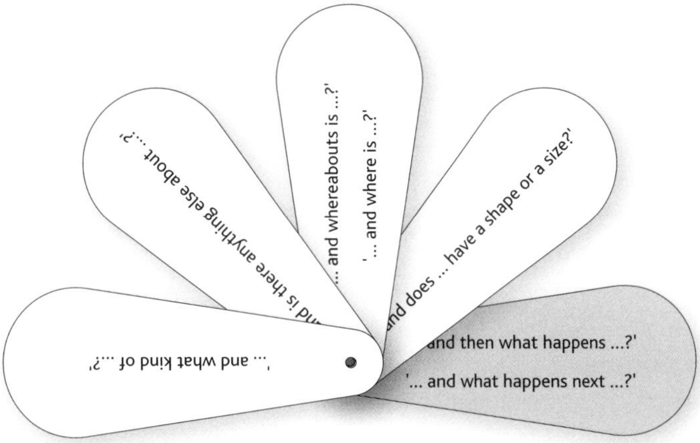
'... and what kind of ...?'
nd is there anything else about ...?'
... and whereabouts is ...?'
'... and where is ...?'
nd does ... have a shape or a size?'
nd then what happens ...?'
'... and what happens next ...?'

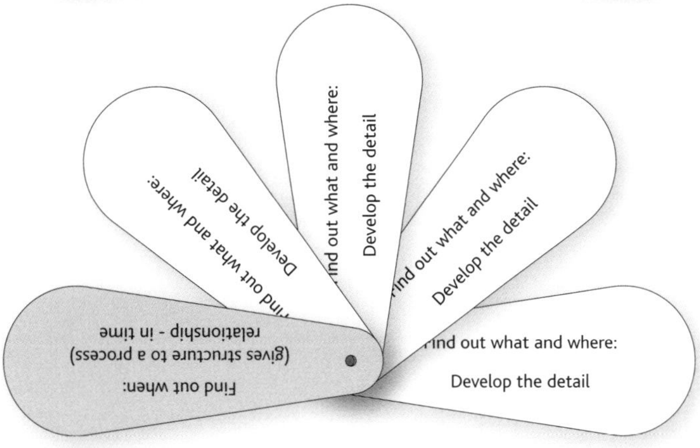
Find out when:
(gives structure to a process)
relationship - in time
ind out what and where:
Develop the detail
ind out what and where:
Develop the detail
ind out what and where:
Develop the detail
ind out what and where:
Develop the detail

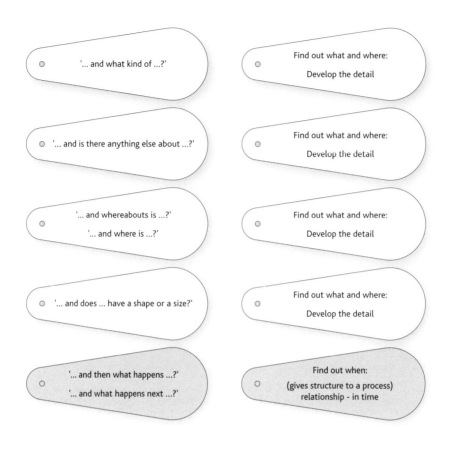

'... and what kind of ...?'

Find out what and where:

Develop the detail

'... and is there anything else about ...?'

Find out what and where:

Develop the detail

'... and whereabouts is ...?'
'... and where is ...?'

Find out what and where:

Develop the detail

'... and does ... have a shape or a size?'

Find out what and where:

Develop the detail

'... and then what happens ...?'
'... and what happens next ...?'

Find out when:

(gives structure to a process)
relationship - in time

# Detail Detective Question Dice

## Dice 1

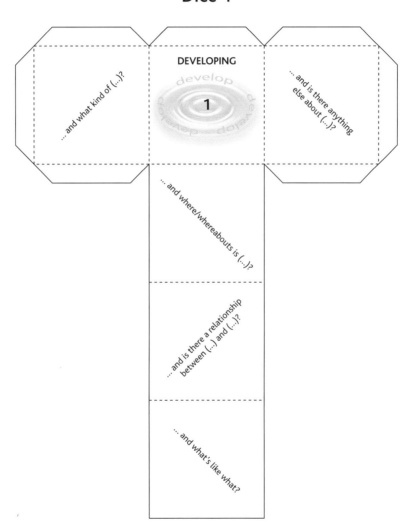

# Dice 2

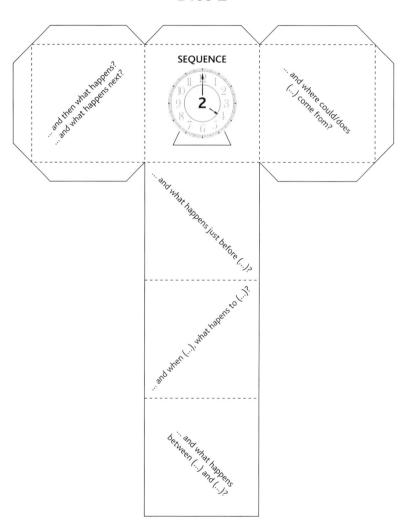

... and then what happens?
... and what happens next?

**SEQUENCE**

2

... and where could/does
(...) come from?

... and what happens just before (...)?

... and when (...), what hapens to (...)?

... and what happens
between (...) and (...)?

# Dice 3

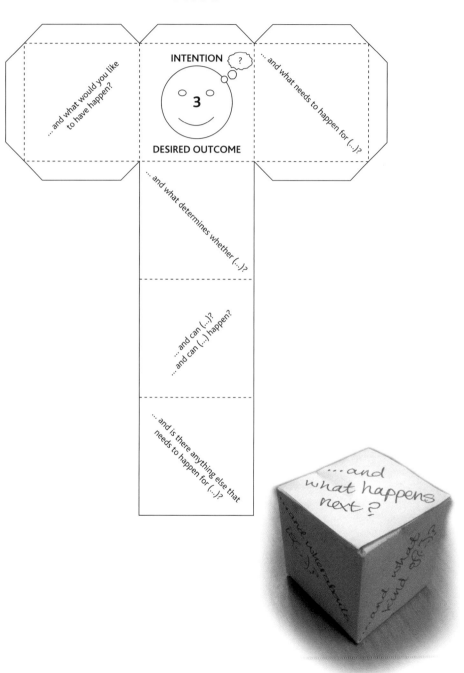

... and what would you like to have happen?

INTENTION

**3**

DESIRED OUTCOME

... and what needs to happen for (...)?

... and what determines whether (...)?

... and can (...)?
and can (...) happen?

... and is there anything else that needs to happen for (...)?

# Appendix F
# Activities and Games

| Group size | Instructions | Resources |
|---|---|---|
| Group or whole-class work | Show and tell. An individual has something to show. The rest of the class/group have one minute to ask only DDQs to find out as much as possible. | An item to show |
| Talk-partner work or occasionally individual work | Be a detective and use the magnifying glass to ask DDQs to find out more. | DDQ magnifying glass (see Appendix B) |
| Individual, group or whole-class work | Make up a story | Story direction cards (see Appendix C) |
| Individual or talk-partner work | Use the DDQ fan to select questions to stimulate thinking and extend knowledge and understanding. | DDQ fan (see Appendix D) |
| Individual, talk-partner or group work | Use one (developing), two (sequence) or three (intention) dice to find out more. | DDQ dice (see Appendix E) |
| Group or whole-class work | Just a minute. One person, or a team, has something in mind. The rest of the class/group has a set time (or a certain number of questions) to ask only DDQs to find out as much as possible. Then they describe, perform, explain or try it on for size – whatever is appropriate to the subject matter – to demonstrate they have guessed it. | Children may choose to take notes |

# Glossary

**Assessment for learning (AfL)** Classroom practices whereby children are encouraged to be active in their learning and to become self-regulated learners, confident and able to learn independently throughout their lives.

**Attribute** A characteristic, aspect, facet, quality or property of something.

**Child centred** Based on a philosophy that children can (and should be) active participants in their own education and development.

**Clean Language** A communications methodology developed by David Grove, a counselling psychologist.

**Clean Set Up** A process developed by Dee Berridge and Caitlin Walker.

**Coaching/coaching approach** Partnering someone in a structured, thought-provoking conversation which serves (through effective listening and questioning) to raise their awareness and inspire them to become clear about their outcomes and generate solutions and strategies to attain them. The process recognises the partner as a capable and whole person who is the expert on 'themselves' and they are challenged and held accountable for their own progress towards their own outcomes.

**Cognitive dissonance** Mental discomfort caused by holding two or more opposing views simultaneously.

**Deep learning** Learning with understanding, where meaning is constructed and connections are made between new and existing ideas and the learner can reason from and apply the learning.

**Desired outcome** What you would like to have happen at/by the end of an occurrence.

**Generative learning** Incorporating existing knowledge with new ideas to gain a better understanding (see Wittrock, 1974).

**Implicit metaphor** Metaphors which imply meaning and/or comparison rather than state it directly (e.g. he was an ox of a man, the house was a fridge).

**Interleaved learning** Introducing new skills alongside previously learned long-term skills to facilitate fast paced learning and/or long-term retention.

**Learning partner** A peer who mutually shares and supports learning through observation, reflection, critical analysis, feedback, encouragement, etc.

**Learning to learn** Where the content of the learning is the process of learning and learners have a choice about which means of learning to apply in different contexts. They engage in metacognition: thinking about thinking (see Bateson, 2000).

**Metacognition** Thinking about thinking – having an awareness and understanding of one's own cognitive process when engaged in learning.

**Metaphor landscape** A system of 'inner world' symbols. The arrangement of these symbols and the relationships between them denotes the structure of a metaphor.

**Necessary conditions** A condition that must be present for an outcome to occur.

**Outcome focus** Where the focus is on the outcome (i.e. the impact or what happens in the end) rather than the means taken to achieve the outcome (i.e. what activities took place). Success is measured by the end result.

**PRO** A model developed by James Lawley and Penny Tompkins to help distinguish between problems, remedies and outcomes.

**Symbol** Something used for, or thought of as, representing something else. It denotes the individual components which make up a metaphor.

**Syntax** The way words or phrases are arranged to form sentences.

**System** A set of related elements (or procedures) which work together to form an integrated whole.

**Talk-partner** see Learning partner.

**Transformative learning** Learning which causes the learner to rethink and reformulate their previous understandings, beliefs and models of the world.

# Bibliography

Angus, J. W. (1981). Children's Conceptions of the Living World. *Australian Science Teachers Journal* 27(3): 65–68.

Bandler, R. and Grinder, J. (1975). *The Structure of Magic, Volume 1* (Palo Alto, CA: Science and Behaviour Books).

Bateson, G. (2000). *Steps to an Ecology of Mind* (Chicago, IL and London: University of Chicago Press).

Bernstein, B. (1971). Education Cannot Compensate for Society. In School and Society Course Team, Open University (ed.), *School and Society* (London: Routledge & Kegan Paul), pp. 61–66.

Biddulph, S. (2010). *Raising Boys: Why Boys Are Different – and How to Help Them Become Happy and Well-Balanced Men* (London: Harper Thorsons).

Biembengut, M. S. (2007). Modelling and Applications in Primary Education. In W. Blum, P. L. Galbraith, H.-W. Henn and M. Niss (eds), *Modelling and Applications in Mathematical Education: The 14th ICMI Study* (New York: Springer), pp. 451–456.

Black, P., Harrison, C., Lee, C., Marshall, B. and Wiliam, D. (2003). *Assessment for Learning: Putting it into Practice* (Maidenhead: Open University Press).

Capra, F. (1988). *Uncommon Wisdom: Conversations with Remarkable People* (New York: Simon & Schuster).

Chambers (2008). *Chambers Dictionary*, 11th edn (Edinburgh: Chambers).

Clarke, S. (2005). *Formative Assessment in Action: Weaving the Elements Together* (London: Hodder).

Corbett, P. (2008). *Talk for Writing Across the Curriculum: How to Teach Non-Fiction Writing 5–12 Years* (Maidenhead: Open University Press).

Csikszentmihalyi, M. (2008). *Flow: The Psychology of Optimal Experience* (New York: HarperCollins).

Dolya, G. (2008). *The Technology of Child Development 'Key to Learning': Vygotskian Approach to Early Education* (Wheathampstead: GDH Publishing).

Doran, G. T. (1981). There's a S.M.A.R.T. Way to Write Management's Goals and Objectives. *Management Review* 70(11): 35–36.

Doyle, J. K. and Ford, D. N. (1998). Mental Models Concepts for System Dynamics Research. *Systems Dynamics Review* 14(1): 3–29.

Dunbar, A. (2010). *Essential Life Coaching Skills* (Hove: Routledge).

Dweck, C. (2007). *Mindset: The New Psychology of Success* (New York: Ballantine Books).

Eerland, A., Guadalupe, T. and Zwaan, R. (2011). Leaning to the Left Makes the Eiffel Tower Seem Smaller: Posture-Modulated Estimation. *Psychological Science* 22(12): 1511–1514.

Fritz, R. (1989). *The Path of Least Resistance* (New York: Fawcett).

Fritz, R. (1991). *Creating* (New York: Fawcett).

Gardner, H. (1991). *The Unschooled Mind* (New York: Basic Books).

Gopnik, A. (2010). How Babies Think. *Scientific American* (July): 76–81. Available at: http://www.alisongopnik.com/papers_alison/sciam-gopnik.pdf.

Grenfell, J. (n.d.). Nursery School [audio]. Available at: http://www.youtube.com/watch?v=ZXhHFgDRNBQ&feature=fvwrel.

Grenfell, J. (n.d.). Nursery School (Going Home) [audio]. Available at: http://www.youtube.com/watch?v=FBFA_AJvrp4.

Grove, D. (1996). And What Kind of Man is David Grove? An Interview by Penny Tompkins and James Lawley, *The Clean Collection*. Available at: http://www.cleanlanguage.co.uk/articles/articles/37/1/And-what-kind-of-a-man-is-David-Grove/Page1.html (first published in *Rapport*, issue 33, August 1996).

Grove, D. (1998). The Philosophy and Principles of Clean Language. Edited by J. Lawley from a talk given at the Clean Language Research Day, London, 13 November, *The Clean Collection*. Available at: http://www.cleanlanguage.co.uk/articles/articles/38/1/Philosophy-and-Principles-of-Clean-Language/Page1.html.

Grove, D. (2003). Summary of David Grove's Ideas – As of 2003, *Clean Language* (29 July). Available at: http://www.cleanlanguage.co.uk/articles/articles/278/1/David-Grove-summary-of-ideas-as-of-2003/Page1.html.

Hattie, J. and Yates, G. (2013). *Visible Learning and the Science of How We Learn* (Abingdon: Routledge).

Holt, J. (1964). *How Children Fail* (New York: Pitman).

Huckle, R. (2013). A New Way of Learning Scales and Arpeggios, *Clean Learning* (14 August). Available at: https://cleanlearning.co.uk/blog/discuss/a-new-way-of-learning-scales-and-arpeggios.

Kline, N. (1999). *Time to Think: Listening to Ignite the Human Mind* (London: Cassell).

Korczak, J. (1920). *How To Love a Child* (Jak kochać dzieci) (Warsaw: n.p.).

Korczak, J. (1992 [1925]). *When I Am Little Again and The Child's Right to Respect*, tr. E. P. Kulawiec, (Lanham, MD: University Press of America).

Lakoff, G. and Johnson, M. (1980). *Metaphors We Live By* (Chicago, IL: Chicago University Press).

Lockhart, P. and Devlin, K. (2009). *A Mathematician's Lament* (New York: Bellevue Literary Press).

Mason, J. with Burton, L. and Stacey, K. (1985). *Thinking Mathematically* (Harlow: Pearson Education).

McGilchrist, I. (2009). *The Master and His Emissary, The Divided Brain and the Making of the Western World* (London and New Haven, CT: Yale University Press).

McGill, B. (2012). *Voice of Reason: Speaking to the Great and Good Spirit of Revolution of Mind* (Sarasota, FL: Paper Lyon Publishing).

McGregor, D. (1960). *The Human Side of Enterprise* (New York: McGraw Hill).

McNerney, S. (2011). A Brief Guide to Embodied Cognition: Why You Are Not Your Brain. *Scientific American Blogs* (4 November). Available at: http://blogs.scientificamerican.com/guest-blog/a-brief-guide-to-embodied-cognition-why-you-are-not-your-brain/.

Moszkowski, A. (1921). *Einstein the Searcher: His Work Explained from Dialogues with Einstein*, tr. H. L. Brose (London: Methuen).

Palmer, S. and Bayley, R. (2013). *Foundations of Literacy*, 4th edn (London: Featherstone Education).

Pask, R. and Joy, B. (2007). *Mentoring-Coaching: A Handbook for Education Professionals* (Milton Keynes: Open University Press).

Penguin (2003). *Penguin English Dictionary*, 2nd edn (London: Penguin).

Petty, G. (2009a). *Evidence Based Teaching: A Practical Approach*, 2nd edn (Cheltenham: Nelson Thornes).

Petty, G. (2009b). *Teaching Today: A Practical Guide* (Cheltenham: Nelson Thornes).

Pinker, S. (2008). *The Stuff of Thought: Language as a Window into Human Nature* (London: Penguin).

Reddy, M. J. (1993). The Conduit Metaphor: A Case of Frame Conflict in Our Language about Language. In A. Ortony (ed.), *Metaphor and Thought* (Cambridge: Cambridge University Press), pp. 164–201.

Robinson, K. with Aronica, L. (2009). *The Element: How Finding Your Passion Changes Everything* (London: Penguin).

Rogers, C. (1983). *Freedom to Learn for the 80's* (Columbus, OH: C.E. Merrill).

Rogers, C. (2004 [1961]). *On Becoming a Person* (London: Constable and Robinson).

Rosenthal, R. (1968). *Pygmalion in the Classroom: Teacher Expectation and Pupils' Intellectual Development* (New York: Holt, Rinehart and Winston).

Salecl, R. (2011). *The Tyranny of Choice* (London: Profile Books).

Schlöglmann, W. (n.d.). Can Neuroscience Help us Better Understand Affective Reactions in Mathematics Learning? Available at: http://www.dm.unipi.it/~didattica/CERME3/proceedings/Groups/TG2/TG2_schloeglmann_cerme3.pdf.

Senge, P., Jaworski, J., Scharmer, C. O. and Flowers, B. S. (2005). *Presence: Exploring Profound Change in People, Organizations and Society* (London: Nicholas Brealey Publishing).

Stephens, J. (1994). *Targeting Students Science Misconceptions: Physical Science Activities Using the Conceptual Change Model* (Riverview, FL: Idea Factory).

Sullivan, W. and Rees, J. (2008). *Clean Language: Revealing Metaphors and Opening Minds* (Carmarthen: Crown House Publishing).

Tompkins, P. and Lawley, J. (2002). *Metaphors in Mind: Transformation through Symbolic Modelling* (London: Developing Company Press).

Tosey, P., Sullivan, W. and Meyer, M. (2013). Clean Sources: Six Metaphors a Minute? University of Surrey. Available at: http://www.cleanchange.co.uk/cleanlanguage/wp-content/uploads/2014/02/Six-metaphors-a-minute-final.pdf.

Walker, C. (2006). *Learning Journeys* [DVD] (Liverpool: John Moores University).

Walker, C. (2014). *From Contempt to Curiosity: Creating the Conditions for Groups to Collaborate Using Clean Language and Systemic Modelling* (Portchester: Clean Publishing).

Way, M. (2010). Clean Gymnastics, *Clean Learning* (14 June). Available at: https://cleanlearning.co.uk/blog/discuss/clean-gymnastics.

Way, M. (2013). *Clean Approaches for Coaches: How to Create the Conditions for Change Using Clean Language and Symbolic Modelling* (Fareham: Clean Publishing).

Williams, L. E. and Bargh, J. A. (2008). Experiencing Physical Warmth Promotes Interpersonal Warmth. *Science* 322(5901): 606–607.

Wittrock, M. C. (1974). Learning As a Generative Process. *Educational Psychologist* 11(2): 87–95.

Za'rour, G. I. (1976). Interpretation of Natural Phenomenon by Lebanese School Children. *Science Education* 60(2): 277–287.

# Using modelling and questioning techniques, Clean Language seeks to improve communication and metacognition in the classroom.

It explores the metaphors that we use and think with, unlocking new levels of understanding. It helps both teachers and learners think about their own thinking and learning, creating deep learning experiences for each child.

Julie McCracken shows teachers how to use Clean Language in their classrooms, including detailed step-by-step instructions, effective questioning and modelling techniques, and case studies.

The benefits of the clean approach include: improved communication; improved attainment; a supportive, collaborative classroom culture; and independent, reflective learners.

A practical and methodological guide to a pedagogical approach which is capable of producing incredible outcomes; not just academically, but in terms of the development of the whole child.

Helen Mulley, editor, *Teach Secondary*

This book could – and should – transform the face of education.

Lynne Cooper, coach, facilitator and trainer, co-author of *The Five-Minute Coach*

This book is concerned with schools; even so, its contents have the potential to inspire and be applied by educators at all levels.

Dr Paul Tosey, independent consultant, Honorary Visiting Fellow, Surrey Business School, University of Surrey

This book will be a great resource for all parents, as well as for educators working with children of any age.

Judy Rees, Clean Language coach, facilitator and trainer, co-author of *Clean Language: Revealing Metaphors and Opening Minds*

An outstanding guide for teachers who want to use questioning strategies.

Richard Churches, Principal Adviser for Research and Evidence Based Practice, Education Development Trust

We highly recommend this book, not only for teachers but for all educators.

James Lawley and Penny Tompkins, authors of *Metaphors in Mind*

Julie McCracken proves that a careful, subtle and humane approach to understanding what is going on in children's heads is not only possible but highly desirable.

Ian Gilbert, founder, Independent Thinking

This is the book for you if you are passionate about transforming the thinking, learning and socialisation of the children you teach, so that they can be their best selves.

Wendy Sullivan, Clean Change Company, co-author of *Clean Language: Revealing Metaphors and Opening Minds*

Julie McCracken is a primary school teacher whose passion for children and effective learning has led her to become a certified Clean Language facilitator and NLP Master Practitioner in addition to her busy day job. She believes in the simple but essential solutions this training provides in allowing her to ensure that her students are part of an inclusive, interactive and happy learning environment.

www.crownhouse.co.uk

ISBN: 978-1845908607

9 781845 908607

Education   Teaching Skills